*Multipitch ice climbing is a great adventure, but it helps to learn to move well on ice first.*

# Climbing:
# From Rock to Ice

# Climbing: From Rock to Ice

## Ron Funderburke

FALCONGUIDES

GUILFORD, CONNECTICUT

## FALCONGUIDES®

An imprint of The Rowman & Littlefield Publishing Group, Inc.
4501 Forbes Blvd., Ste. 200
Lanham, MD 20706
www.rowman.com
Falcon and FalconGuides are registered trademarks and Make
Adventure Your Story is a trademark of The Rowman & Littlefield
Publishing Group, Inc.

Distributed by NATIONAL BOOK NETWORK

Photos by Ron Funderburke, except where noted.

British Library Cataloguing in Publication Information available

**Library of Congress Cataloging-in-Publication Data available**

ISBN 978-1-4930-2762-0 (paperback)
ISBN 978-1-4930-2763-7 (e-book)

∞™ The paper used in this publication meets the minimum
requirements of American National Standard for Information
Sciences—Permanence of Paper for Printed Library Materials,
ANSI/NISO Z39.48-1992.

# Contents

# Introduction

Some seasoned rock climbers might enjoy endless summers, halcyon days, and they may never worry about the cold dark days of winter. For some, there is simply no such thing as winter. They winter in Joshua Tree, summer at higher elevations, and fill their springs and falls with road trips to sunny crags, boulders, and big walls.

Some seasoned rock climbers might gracefully dance up sunny slabs and faces, flowing through moves on sure-footed smears and crisp edges. They find harmony and balance in every inch of movement, leaving no more trace than a falling feather. Even on those days when they struggle and grunt for every millimeter of an off width, they know that the rock cannot change its essential character, unlike the mutable climber that labors beneath it.

This book is not for those rock climbers.

They won't appreciate what we have in store for them. This book is for the rock climber who mournfully watches the first snows of winter blanket her crags, the ice sealing off her finger crack projects; they wonder how they will survive a winter without climbing something beautiful, something incomparable, something inspiring.

This book is for the climber that wants to turn the tables on the climbing medium for once. For the climber that wants to climb something impermanent, to carve and sculpt the climbing surface, to pretend for one small second that the climber is both the unmovable object and the unstoppable force.

***There is always finesse in ice climbing, but there is also unapologetic destruction.***

This book is for the climber that wants to be more than a floating feather, a climber that yearns for some noise, some percussion, some action to disrupt, to disturb, to destroy the climb as she climbs it. Ice climbing is all those things, and for all the things it has in common with rock climbing, it is most definitely *not* rock climbing.

Ice climbing takes everything that's enjoyable about rock climbing and extends the argument. If you love toys and tools, ice climbing has all the same toys and tools as rock climbing, but adds countless new gadgets and trinkets. If you love the aesthetic quality of rock faces, then ice climbs adorn those places in ways that you will want to experience more intimately. If you love soaring and sailing movement, ice climbing offers sweeping gestures of the limbs, scaling terrain in spans only limited by the length of an ice ax on the tips of your fingers. If nothing else, ice climbing gives you something novel to do in the winter.

In the chapters to follow, we'll equip an experienced rock climber with the tools and techniques to begin their ice climbing career. It doesn't really matter why a climber chooses to ice climb, or what purpose ice climbing serves in their climbing; the stipulation of this book is that rock climbing is a natural precursor to ice climbing. As many climbers will attest, ice climbing is entirely avoidable for rock climbers, but we don't know of many circumstances where rock climbing is entirely avoidable for ice climbers or alpinists. This central idea grounds the work we hope to do in this book. If your heart's desire is ice climbing, learn to rock climb. Read the other books in our series, work with a climbing instructor or guide, lay a foundation for your ice climbing before continuing with the rest of this book.

# CHAPTER ONE

# Defining Ice Climbing

In this book, we're going to stick to the kinds of ice climbing experiences and locations that make effective transitions from rock climbing to ice climbing. Ice climbing can take adventurous climbers to some remote, frigid, and outlandish places—but those are not the best places to learn to ice climb. When a climber first begins to transition from rock to ice, single-pitch ice crags offer the best environments for learning. In time, when one has learned to climb ice efficiently, to lead and share leads, remote multipitch ice climbs, or alpine climbs will surely beckon. For now, we need more of a classroom setting.

In this chapter, we're going to devote some time to defining single-pitch ice cragging. We're not going to discuss multipitch ice. We're not going to explore ice climbs that draw the climbing team into alpine terrain, or terrain with long approaches, glaciers, or exposure to avalanche conditions. We're also going to stay away from too much mixed climbing or drytooling. Mixed climbing and drytooling are remarkable climbing activities, but they are so unlike ice climbing, we would need quite a bit more time and text to dive into a proper explanation of the discipline. In this book, when crampons or ice tools touch the rock, it will only be incidental to an ice climb. We will not focus on extensive rock work.

*Drytooling is a specialized form of winter climbing where tools and crampons focus on climbing rock instead of ice.*

| Ice climbing in this book | Winter climbing not in this book |
| --- | --- |
| Waterfall ice climbs | Glacier ice, alpine ice, or snow climbs. Rime ice or splash ice. |
| Swinging technical ice tools into waterfall ice | Using a mountain ax or drytooling |
| Easy approaches | Alpine approaches over glaciers or extensive 4th class terrain |
| Safe established approaches | Terrain that requires avalanche safety and awareness |
| Single pitch with permanent anchors | Multipitch ice |
| WI1-6 difficulties. See ice climbing grades chart. | WI7. Ice climbs with dangerous protection. |

*Mixed climbing combines drytooling and ice climbing, but this book will not explore mixed climbing extensively.*

Similarly, this book will focus on waterfall ice, not alpine ice. It might sound simplistic, but waterfall ice differs from other forms of ice in the mountains. It feels different when it is climbed. It protects differently, relying more heavily on ice screws than snow pickets or other forms of snow protection. Waterfall ice is formed when liquid water freezes. It tends to be translucent, whereas alpine ice is opaque because it is formed by compressed and consolidated snow. When an ice ax pick penetrates waterfall ice, the ice cracks and breaks, like slamming the pick into glass,

*Ice that forms when liquid water freezes is called waterfall ice or water ice.*

*Ice that forms by compressing snow looks different. It's more common on alpine climbs, not frozen waterfalls.*

whereas alpine ice just seems to make room for the pick, like slamming the pick into Styrofoam. The sound waterfall ice makes when struck or kicked is a crack and a snap. Meanwhile, alpine ice tends to squeak and chirp.

We'll also avoid some of the remarkable ice formed by glaciers. Intrepid ice climbers have explored mind-bending caves of ice in the dry parts of glaciers. The deep blue ice in the bellies of glaciers is a truly amazing thing to behold, but to see it and climb it, you've got to cross glaciers and other complex alpine terrain. Our book will stick to the ice flows that come inching down frozen crags all over the country every winter.

We will also avoid talking too much about rime ice or splash ice. When the air temperature is so suddenly cold that it freezes water vapor to any exposed surface, everything in the world can be covered in rime ice. Climbers in Scotland's peaks and high fells have made an art of climbing the thinnest layers of rime ice, but the techniques they use look and feel more like mixed rock and ice climbing than pure

*Glacier ice can form wondrous shapes, but you have to get to some wild places to see those shapes.*

*Rime ice can coat rock surfaces so thoroughly it can be climbed, but a climber often has to make extensive use of drytooling techniques when rime is involved.*

waterfall ice climbing. So, we'll avoid rime. Splash ice forms when high-volume waterfalls kick up so much spray into the air that adjacent rock faces form huge sheets of splash ice and hundreds of hanging daggers. With each sub-freezing day that passes and each molecule of water that swells and fattens these overhanging ice gardens, otherworldly ice dungeons are formed—but splash ice can be inconsistent. Some sections have formed and adhered to the rock surface so perfectly that ice screws can be securely drilled, and they may even hold falls. Other sections chip away and break so easily that movement feels more like whack-a-mole than waterfall ice climbing. Splash ice is too unpredictable and usually too hard for most ice climbers to enjoy.

## Waterfall Ice Climbs

Creeks and drainages usually supply the water that freezes into ice climbs, but they can also be formed by seeps in porous rock surfaces. Some ice climbs consistently form because layers of rock have been blasted away to form roads or tunnels. These road-cut ice flows form consistently because the water that might otherwise be flowing from vegetation to topsoil is now cascading over a recently exposed rock face. The formation of ice usually confers the difficulty of the ice climbing, the number grade used to describe the climbing difficulty. Once an ice climber learns where and how ice climbs form, it's easier to anticipate which terrain features will produce ice climbs and how hard they will be.

| Ice climbing grade | What the grade means |
|---|---|
| WI1 | Low-angled ice, like a frozen ramp. If tools are used at all, they are used like a cane or walking stick. |
| WI2 | Low-angled ice, but at least one tool is occasionally used in traction to clear small bulges. The crampons can typically be flat-footed at any time. |
| WI3 | Short vertical sections of one or two body lengths. Both tools are used in traction position throughout. Crampons are front-pointed throughout, but flat-footed for rests. |
| WI4 | Longer vertical sections of three to four body lengths with rests in between strenuous sections. Overlapping ice curtains or daggers may create short overhangs. |
| WI5 | Sustained vertical sections with few rests. Overlapping ice curtains or daggers may create short overhangs. Thin ice or verglas may preclude kicking with crampons or swinging ice tools. |
| WI6 | Overlapping ice curtains or daggers may create overhangs of any size, with sustained vertical ice climbing throughout. Rests are unavailable. Thin ice or verglas may preclude kicking with crampons or swinging ice tools; sometimes only the lightest taps are possible. Thin columns may require very delicate climbing. |

# Ice Climb Profiles

## WI1. Frozen Creek Hikes

Waterfall Ice 1 ice climbs are great treasures. They typically form on low volume creeks. They are so low angled that they get covered in snow quickly during winter storms, so it's nice to find a good WI1 before it's buried. The bare and visible ice is part of the enjoyment of climbing a WI1.

These climbs provide aspiring ice climbers opportunities to explore ice with a primary focus on crampon placements and footwork. An ice climber can quietly ascend a frozen creek, take in the wintry scenery, and focus each step on getting to know how crampons work. Short uphill steps or benches in the creek allow an ice climber practice front pointing. One tool in hand lets an ice climber make a few traction swings here and there. It wouldn't be a terrible idea to use a rope to belay terrain like this, but WI1 is usually travelled without a rope. Easy does it, though. A slip could turn into a slide that would be very difficult to stop.

For a rock climber, WI1 should feel like climbing 4th class. It's unlikely that a climber would fall, but rushing, inattentiveness, or complacency could result in an unfortunate incident.

## WI2. Frozen Slabs

Long slabby creek and river beds or any rock slab that runs with water will form WI2 ice climbs. Long low-angled creek and river beds are not steeper than your average hillside. They form great classrooms for learning to move with crampons. Frozen creek or river beds or any rock slab with water will form WI2 ice climbs. These slabs can usually be climbed with a single ice

*Gently sloping ice slabs let an ice climber practice front pointing.*

tool and crampons, but suddenly the size and steepness of the slab makes a rope feel like an absolute necessity to prevent fall consequences. These climbs primarily make an ice climber focus on footwork, combining a flat-footed stance with a front point. As the climber encounters short waist to chest high bulges, an ice tool is needed to surmount the steeper features. While it's true that the climber never feels that upper-body fatigue that's characteristic of ice climbing at higher grades, the feet and legs get a strong workout, for sure.

For a rock climber, WI2 should feel like low-grade-5th class climbing. It should not feel difficult to climb, but just like the high stakes of a 5th-class rock climb, the hazards merit roped protection, regardless of how likely a fall feels.

## *WI3. Vertical Ice Primer*

WI3 ice climbs present vertical sections that are one or two body lengths high, so they are great climbs to hone vertical ice climbing technique. A climber can practice creating a firm foundation for the first tool placement, then placing a second tool placement. Even though the fun will be over quickly, these short vertical sections are when the rhythm of ice climbing can be engrained.

WI3 climbs let an ice climber practice front pointing with both feet and using ice tools in traction positions.

For a rock climber, WI3 should feel like entry-level rock climbing, like 5.4 to 5.6. There may be moves where the climber is glad to have a rope, but the rests are so frequent it's hard to get over-pumped.

## WI4. Vertical Ice

Having learned the rhythm and technique of vertical ice climbing on WI3, longer vertical sections put those skills to the test. These steep columns and ice faces

*Longer vertical icefalls let an ice climber practice front pointing with both feet, using both ice tools in traction, and moving efficiently to manage severe fatigue.*

force a climber to develop stamina, to find creative stemming opportunities to avert fatigue, and to rest wisely before sustained vertical challenges. The first impressively steep features an ice climber will climb happen at WI4.

For a rock climber, WI4 should feel like moderate rock, 5.7–5.9. Sure, there are difficulties. Sure, it takes some good technique and some stamina, but most rock climbers who routinely climb moderate grades can build up to WI4 ice climbing.

## WI5. The Barrier Grade

WI5 is the difficulty where the most dramatic daggers, columns, and smears come sailing down from above. If a climber had managed to thug their way up WI4 with poor technique, it will be unlikely for them to maintain that strategy at WI5 and above. WI5 climbs necessitate a combination of physical ice climbing fitness, sound technique, and creative problem solving. It's also the first grade that will demand a climber to think about and manage muscular fatigue in their extremities. A WI5 climber will learn to find stems and rests to take weight off their arms. They'll learn to shake out and alleviate the burn of lactic acid buildup in the forearms.

For a rock climber, WI5 will feel like 5.10. It's an equivalent barrier grade. It will be difficult for someone with tons of fitness but no technique to climb a varied 5.10 trad climb. At 5.10, technique and fitness combine to create fluid movement, fatigue management, and overall movement efficiency. Similarly, WI5 brings all the techniques of a seasoned ice climber into play, and it reveals the weaknesses of an unseasoned ice climber.

*WI5 climbs are vertical for longer distances, so stamina and technique have to come together.*
Photo courtesy of Colorado Mountain School.

## *WI6. Ice Gets Weird and Hard*

WI6 doesn't have a clean comparison to rock climbing. It's just weird and hard. For the leader, weird and hard also means dangerous. There are WI6 climbs that are just so steep and sustained that the only strategy is to be really fit, climb really efficiently, and move without

*WI6 climbs combine all of an ice climber's fitness, courage, and finesse. They're rarely climbed with pure strength.*

As a young ice climber, I wanted to climb WI5 and WI6 difficulties. It was my goal. I had climbed and successfully led all the WI4s I had tried, but I also got flaming pumped when I toproped WI5. I was scared to lead climbs at that level because I couldn't wrap my head around leading a climb that I could barely top-rope. At that time, I was regularly onsighting 5.11 trad climbs, I had redpointed plenty of 5.12s, and I had a conviction that I was fit enough to climb WI5. Why couldn't I do it? Convinced that my problem involved stamina, I started these long endurance workouts on my back porch. Hanging on my ice tools, alternating hands, clipping a quickdraw on and off of a bolt that was placed on an adjacent wall. Still, I could not get up a WI5 without getting cross-eyed pumped. Finally, I spent a day climbing with a mentor, and he offered me a casual question, not feedback, not advice, just a question: "Why do you skip all the rests?" I didn't understand the question. "What rests?" Up to that point, I only perceived rests as places where I fully take my hand off of my tools. My mentor said, "Look, I know you're in great climbing shape right now, probably better shape than me even, but watch me climb this same climb. I'm going to show you the rests you're skipping." I watched in disbelief as he repeatedly stemmed his feet to adjacent columns, daggers, and rock features. At each stemming rest, he was able to casually hold one tool while he shook out, one arm and then the other, turning around and narrating his recovery to me while he achieved it. It was a huge conceptual leap for me. Technique is how you manage the pump. Of course, the fitness helps, but eventually, ice climbing reaches a difficulty where stubborn muscles are not adequate. Fitness has to be accompanied by thoughtfulness, patience, and problem solving, just like in rock climbing. You can't climb a WI5 simply by gaining more muscles. I started leading WI5s within the same week.

hesitation or deliberation. On other climbs, there are sections that are so delicate and insecure, it's hard to say that technique and stamina are not in play, but they are only as important as overall poise and gumption.

For a rock climber, WI6 will probably feel like climbing 5.10+ choss. On a chossy rock climb, the individual move will feel like 5.10, but the care needed to find and use the good holds not the bad holds, to recycle handholds as footholds, to carefully avoid nudging loose rocks off the pitch, to endure the mental taxation of so much added difficulty without reprieve; that's kind of what WI6 feels like. It's not a one-for-one comparison, but as we covered, there is no one-for-one comparison between rock climbing and WI6 ice climbing. It's more about being comfortable with hyper focusing, demanding physical difficulty, and wildly imaginative movement.

## Using Guidebooks and Online Resources

An experienced rock climber will be very familiar with the use of guidebooks and online resources like Mountain Project. These resources will produce all the same planning and preparation information for an ice climb that a rock climber would find useful on any rock climb. Pay special attention to aspect. North-facing ice climbs tend to form reliably, but their northern aspect means an ice-cold day for the climbing team. Make note of aspect as it relates to wind direction too. Windy conditions can turn a cold day into a hellish experience. Use route research to plan all the climbing team's necessities, like food and water, clothing, emergency preparedness and

*When an ice climb is not in the cards it's better to come back another day, which can be disappointing after a long approach.*

communication, rack, rope, and anchor requirements, popularity and social aspects of the climb. An experienced rock climber will be accustomed to gathering all this information. Check out the research checklists in the appendix of this book for a reminder of the kinds of information you'll want to gather when you are studying a new climb or climbing area.

*This waterfall could be seen from a distance, but upon arrival it was clear that the left side had not yet formed. Good to know for the next time.*

For ice climbing, it's just as important to study conditions as it is to study guidebooks and online resources. It's not very useful to know that an ice climb forms on a given feature at certain times of year. The real question is whether or not the climb is formed on the day that you want to climb it. There are a few main tactics for discovering conditions.

**Blind Conditions Onsight.** If the air temperature is below freezing, and it hasn't risen above freezing in a few days, there's probably ice. If you and your

The local scout. Every ice climbing community in the country has an intrepid ice hound somewhere in the pack. This character just loves playing and exploring, alone or with friends, and she/ he loves to share their discoveries with the community. If you want to know about conditions, you want to know this person. In my case, I quickly made the acquaintance of Josh Whitmore, when I lived in western North Carolina. As a pro cyclist and all-around aerobic bad-ass, Josh was constantly exploring the terrain in the densely forested mountains. He always seemed to know the condition of every ice climb, no matter how far from the road it was located.

partner are willing to risk a cold hike, regardless of the ice climbing outcome, a blind conditions onsight might be worth your time. Don't waste time researching, calling locals, calling guides, or scouting. Just hike in there. If the climb is there, climb it. If it's not, don't. No problem. You got a nice hike in. Also, you just logged a data point about that ice climb that will be useful in the future. The next time that same weather pattern presents itself, you'll have a stronger idea about whether or not your ice climb will be there.

**Scouting.** Climbers with a penchant for trail running often enjoy scouting. They'll assemble a very light kit, jog in to their intended climb, scout the conditions, snap some photos, and jog out. If ice climbs are local, even long approaches can be quickly dispatched at a running pace. Scouting is not an option for everyone, but someone has to do it. Otherwise, where do all the conditions reports come from?

**Conditions Reporting.** In years past, every local ice climbing community relied on a small pack of ice hounds to know the condition of every icicle forming on every climb within 100 square miles of their homes. If you knew that climber, or you knew someone who knew that climber, conditions reports were just a phone call away. These ice hounds were usually local guides, or just avid local ice climbers who spend a lot of free time bird-dogging ice formations. In both cases, they had an incentive to know whether the ice was in: They wanted to climb it after work or they wanted to climb it at work.

Nowadays, social media has made it easy to check conditions of ice climbing areas, specific ice climbs, even ice climb unicorns that only form once in a decade. You can engage with these conditions forums

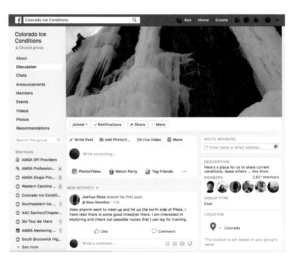

*Social media and open forums give ice climbers an opportunity to scout conditions and share conditions they find throughout a winter season.*

passively, scrolling through other people's reporting until you find the photo or comment that answers your question. Or, you can engage actively, posting an inquiry about the area or the climb of interest. If any climber has had eyes on your prize, you'll likely receive a comment or a qualified speculation quickly. If you go climbing, regardless of what you find, it's also helpful to post your own conditions report. Whether you use the forum actively or passively, share the conditions you find. If no one ever shares, there is no forum.

# CHAPTER TWO

# Rock Climbing Review

B ecoming an experienced and thoughtful rock climber before becoming an ice climber is an advantageous progression. It has some drawbacks, like movement, but the advantages far outnumber the disadvantages. Most conspicuously, ice climbing is a cold activity that happens during the shortest days of the year. The environment and the time pressures create an environment where it is easy to be hasty, to overlook key steps and double-checks, where it can be difficult to make clear-headed decisions.

Imagine trying to learn nuanced technical skills like ropecraft, anchoring, and lead climbing in the midst of harsh environmental conditions. It would be a hostile learning environment, for sure. By contrast, a rock climber has already engrained most of the ropecraft needed to ice climb. She already has a firm understanding of sound anchoring principles. She already understands the dynamics involved in lead climbing, and she knows how to protect a climb to mitigate impact hazards.

When her fingers are numb and the end of the day is rapidly approaching, she'll be glad she doesn't have to figure out how to rappel. She'll be glad she has already practiced the rigging, the double-checks, and the communication with her partner. She'll spend her ice climbing career focusing on lessons unique to the medium, and she'll be less likely to be sidelined by technical skills that could've been honed in a T-shirt on a sunny crag, or even in the gym.

In this chapter, we'll briefly review a few key skill sets from rock climbing that are directly reflected in ice climbing so that subsequent chapters can focus on aspects of ice climbing that are truly unique. Specifically, we'll review fundamentals of ropecraft, belaying, anchoring, lead climbing, and rappelling.

## Ropecraft

Knots and hitches, rope management, and all the contortions of the climbing rope do not change that much in ice climbing. Most climbers tie in with a Figure 8 Follow Through, and the dressing and

*Tying knots and hitches, anchoring, and rope management are all familiar skills for a rock climber.*

| Ropecraft | Most Common Applications | Unique Ice Climbing Concerns |
|---|---|---|
| **Knots** | | |
| Figure 8 Follow Through | Tying the climber to the end of the rope. | Gloved hands feel clumsy at first, even though the knot is so familiar. Smooth dry-treated ropes have to be tightened with extra care. They're slippery. |
| Stopper Knots | Knotting a rope-end | The slippery ropes mean that stopper knots need to be cinched down tight. |
| Flat Overhand | Tying a master point | UHMWP cords and slings are thinner than their nylon brothers. The skinny slings can be difficult to untie with gloved hands. |
| **Hitches** | | |
| Clove Hitch | Connecting a climber to an anchor with a locking carabiner | Frozen ropes make hitches behave oddly. A stiff rope can reduce the Clove Hitch's strength. |
| Munter Hitch | Direct belaying | Munter Hitches can sometimes be the only belay technique that will work on icy/frozen ropes. |
| Autoblock Friction Hitch | Backing up rappels and lowers | An iced prussic loop can make the autoblock slip unexpectedly. |
| Prussic Friction Hitch | Improvised rescue sequences, rope ascension, load transfers | All friction hitches can be affected by icy prussic loops. |
| **Rope Management** | | |
| Rope Stack | Managing a rope at a stance, prepping a rope for belaying | Slippery ropes on slippery ledges mean that rope stacks can tumble and fall. They must be stacked and patted down carefully. |
| Coils | Transporting a rope | Frozen ropes can be difficult to coil. |

symmetry of a well-tied 8 make it recognizable to an ice climber's eyes just like it would to a rock climber. Any climber attached to a climbing rope can anchor that climbing rope with a Clove Hitch just as reliably on a sub-zero icefall as sunny sandstone. An Autoblock

*It's very difficult to tie a friction hitch with a nylon loop that is frozen solid. Even if it's tied, the ice can affect the hitch's grip.*

*When ropes get wet and then freeze, they can be stiff and difficult. Some hitches won't bind as tightly.*

*The faithful Figure 8 Follow Through can loosen and shift when ropes are stiff and frozen.*

Friction Hitch makes a nice backup for rappels and lowers, while a Prussic Friction Hitch grabs the rope tightly and predictably. Rope-ends that need to be untied frequently can still be connected with a Flat Overhand, even though the Double Fisherman's is a stronger bend. The one is still useful when the bend needs to be untied immediately (like rappelling), and the other is still valuable for connections that will be more permanent (like cords and prussic loops).

# Belaying

The fundamentals of belaying do not change in an ice climbing medium. A constant brake hand, hand transitions in a position of maximum friction, and use of the body and limbs' natural strength apply to all

*A frozen rope can make it difficult to use an autoblocking belay device.*

*With so much icefall, Assisted Braking Devices give the belayer a much-needed margin of error.*

| Belay Context | Unique Ice Climbing Concerns |
|---|---|
| Counterweight belay of a toprope with a Manual Braking Device (MBD) | Icefall is common and predictable. Using backup belayers or the use of backup knots is prudent. |
| Counterweight belay of a toprope with an Assisted Braking Device (ABD) | Mechanical ABDs can freeze or jam. Passive designs are less susceptible to freezing issues. |
| Counterweight lead belaying | All the same ABD and MBD concerns apply to a lead belay in a counterweight context. Passive ABDs give the team a margin of error. |
| Direct belay of a second | Icy ropes can be difficult to move through a belay tool. It's good to keep the Munter Hitch handy when ropes are icy. |
| Running belays | Simul-climbing in an environment with so much overhead impact hazard (icefall) can be especially hazardous. |
| Firefighter's belays | Firefighter's belays often put the belayer directly underneath icefall from the rappeller. |

*Mechanical Assisted Braking Devices, like the Grigi™, can freeze. Instead, passive Assisted Braking Devices are more reliable in freezing conditions.*

belay tools, belay hitches, and belay contexts. We still prioritize vigilance; we're still appreciative of a finite attention span and the need to give the belay team a margin of error; we still adapt to new belay tools, counterweight belays, and direct belays.

## Anchoring

Anchoring in ice climbing reinforces the same fundamentals of strength, security, and simplicity. Anchors still need to be strong enough to hold all potential loads the climbing team could conceivably create and provide a margin of error in overall load-bearing capacity. Anchors still need to be secure; they still need to be able to withstand the failure of a single part of the system. Anchors still need to be simple. Anchor builders still need to reconcile anchor construction with a finite amount of time and material; they still need to prioritize solving the anchoring challenge in a way that is not unnecessarily

*With a pair of reliable modern bolts, a pair of locker draws make an excellent and quick anchor.*

*Since toprope setups often protect multiple fall lines, due to directional placements down on the pitch, a self-adjusting anchor system will accommodate several ice climbs from one anchor.*

complicated or time-consuming. Ice climbing basically introduces the possibility of anchoring in ice with v-threads, slung columns, and ice screws. Mostly, these techniques are the purview of multipitch ice climbing, which we won't address in this book. However, the same principles would apply to those anchors. In single-pitch ice climbing, anchors will

*Trees are useful for anchoring rock climbs and ice climbs.*

*Static rope anchors help collate components that are far apart from each other. This skill set is just as useful for ice climbs as rock.*

look very familiar because they will involve the same bolts, trees, and permanent anchors that rock climbers configure continuously.

# Lead Climbing

Any trad climber will quickly understand the stakes of leading ice. Trad climbers have likely faced and overcome sections of rock climbs where the leader could not find ample protection, where the leader was forced to use poise, focus, and movement ability

*Body-length distribution of protection is a reasonable measure of a well-protected ice lead.*

*When protection is too frequent, it is exhausting to place, and equally exhausting to remove. This frequency actually makes a fall more likely.*

to avoid falling at all costs. In scenarios like that, the leader would likely have survived the massive fall they would have taken, but the uncertainty and likelihood of injury made the stakes of falling too high.

Leading ice feels like that all the time. Even if a leader protects a pitch conservatively, placing ice screws every half-body length, six- to ten-foot falls on ice present the same uncertainty as rock climbs of

*With protection this infrequent, one has to wonder why the leader bothers at all. The consequences of a fall would be similar if he were free soloing.*

three times the length. The presence of crampons and ice axes increases the likelihood of injury. A crampon can catch a single point, and the falling leader's mass can easily snap a bone, sprain a joint, or tear soft tissues. Impalements can easily happen.

As a result, ice climbing leaders tend to climb with the same poise and focus, determined and stable movement, that a rock climber uses on runout sections. The ice climber protects a pitch so that they will survive a fall if it happens, but their primary tactic is to avoid falling.

An ice climbing leader also has to think very carefully about the exposure of the climbing team to freezing conditions. Over protecting a pitch exposes the leader and the belayer for a longer period of time. Under protecting a pitch might be faster, but it also increases fall distances and the likelihood of severe or lethal injuries. Unlike runout rock climbs, ice leaders can usually place as much protection as they wish, but how much and how often is usually a complex risk-management calculation.

## Rappelling

Rappelling down an ice climb is no less treacherous than a rock climb. Use of backups is still critical. Being secure as the rappeller transitions from one safety system to the next is still an imperative. Managing the

A quick upward tug "challenges" the friction hitch.

*Since friction hitches can be covered with snow and ice particles, it's wise to "challenge" the hitch before trusting it. Give the rope a quick tug to make sure the hitch engages.*

Clean rappel rig: rope ends managed, friction hitch backup, extension.

*Rappelling is just as dangerous in ice climbing as rock climbing. The use of extensions, backups, and managed rope-ends are valuable habits.*

ends of the rope for every rappel still helps prevent a rappeller from rappelling off the ends of the rope.

In ice climbing, the frozen medium should present a healthy skepticism to the use of friction hitches and firefighter's belays in particular. They're both still valuable techniques, but the rappeller that insists on challenging the systems prior to implementation is a rappeller that appreciates the effects of snow and ice on soft goods.

Similarly, a firefighter's belay is a valuable tool for giving a rappeller a backup, but the belayer is often positioned directly underneath the fall line of the rappeller. The belay can be hazardous because the rappeller can accidentally kick ice down on the belayer. For firefighter's belays on ice, it's wise to step back slightly out of the rappeller's fall line, but still in a position to affect a braking action should the rappeller lose control.

# CHAPTER THREE

# Equipment

I ce climbing equipment enlists a long list of tools, apparel, and unique modifications that are unique to this particular style of climbing. Rock climbing apparel doesn't quite work for ice climbing, and the winter wear most skiers and cold-weather enthusiasts accumulate doesn't quite work either. The bulky insulated boots that protect and insulate feet during most winter activities don't quite do the job for ice climbing. The gloves that we might use to shovel snow are not quite nimble enough. The harnesses, the belay hardware, the supplies and extras: They all have to be recalibrated, adjusted, or replaced when we go ice climbing.

It can be frustrating for someone to look at this daunting list of new equipment and apparel. So this text will focus on a steady transition, in which we delay major purchases through an experimental and exploratory phase, a first-time ice climber phase. Then, once a climber is ready to make the plunge, we'll explore the very first ice climbing kit, when the unique essentials to ice climbing are purchased and personalized. Lastly, we'll explore how a climber might diversify their equipment as their needs, abilities, and desires evolve and expand.

## Phase 1: First-Time Ice Climber

The very first time you venture out on an ice climb, you'll want to dig up a few winter apparel items that

Rock climbing
harness and helmet

Ski pants, jacket,
and gloves

Borrowed
ice tools
and crampons

Snow boots

you probably already own. If you don't own a pair of winter gloves, waterproof snow pants and parka, or other winter outdoor necessities, then you can pick and choose how you skip ahead to a purchasing phase of equipment acquisition. If snow pants cost you $100 and an ice climbing pant would also cost $100, it might make sense for those ice climbing pants to be your snow pants, regardless of your fate as an ice climber.

There is an assumption here that most of us who have rock climbed and spent time outside when it's cold will already own versions of this equipment and apparel to try ice climbing for the first time.

| If you already have… | Modify it for ice climbing by… | Make note of the following for later purchases. |
|---|---|---|
| **Winter Apparel and Accessories** | | |
| **Waterproof pants.** Rain pants over non-cotton pants, insulated snow pants over long underwear. | Remove everything from pockets. | Baggy pants can snag, and the climber feels less nimble. Pay attention to how an athletic fit would feel better. Also, pay attention to the material; if it's too sweaty, you might want a more breathable material. |
| **Waterproof coat/jacket/parka.** A raincoat over non-cotton layers. A ski jacket. A durable puffy jacket. | Empty the pockets so the jacket can tuck underneath your harness. | Does the hood cover your helmet? Make note. Do you have more pockets than you need? Does the jacket stay tucked underneath the harness? |
| **Gloves.** Ski gloves. A durable winter work glove. | Give the gloves a quick waterproof treatment. | Can you use your fingertips? Can you feel your fingers sliding inside the glove when you grip the tool? Is the glove fabric slippery? |
| **Warm hat** | Try on the hat and helmet combo before you leave the house. Make all the necessary adjustments. | Does the hat and helmet combination feel too warm? Too itchy? Can you hear your partners? |
| **Boots.** Snow boots. Sturdy hiking boots with warm socks. Ski or snowboard boots. | Try on crampons with boots before leaving the house. Make all the necessary adjustments to crampons and boots. | Does the crampon stay flat against the bottom of your foot? Can you feel your foot flexing in and out of the crampon? Does the crampon cut off the circulation in your toes? Did you bang your toes in the front of the boot? |

## Climbing Gear

| | | |
|---|---|---|
| **Helmet** | Adjust helmet fit to include a warm hat. | Did you sustain a lot of ice impacts? Did you damage your helmet? |
| **Harness** | Make sure harness fits over all of your outer layers. Add wiregate carabiners as temporary ice clippers. | Did the girth of the all the extra clothing make the harness uncomfortable or non-functional? |
| **Hardware** | Leave mechanical Assisted Braking Device at home. | Did carabiners ice up or become non-functional in the cold? Were any tools difficult to use with gloves? |
| **Soft goods (slings, rope, and cords)** | Bundle and coil soft goods more compactly. They snag on crampons when you kneel. | Did nylon materials freeze? Were they too stiff to use? |
| **Ice climbing gear to share or borrow** | If you have mountaineering boots, ice tools and crampons can be shared. | Try more than one brand. You'll need to borrow from a few different friends on a few different outings. |
| **Ice tools** | Adjust personal sizing | Decide if higher-end performance tools are really necessary. If not, a modest all-arounder might be just right. |
| **Crampons** | Adjust personal sizing | Decide if higher-end performance crampons are really necessary. If not, a modest all-arounder might be just right. |

## First-Time Crampons

You first ice climbing trip is likely to acquaint you with some of the variations in crampon design. If you are putting a crampon over a hiking boot, for example, you will likely be unable to use a technically fitting crampon, the kind that has a toe bail and a heel lever. Odds are, you'll be using some adjustable straps to hold the crampon onto your heel and toe. If you are using a ski boot, you might be able to make a technical crampon work. Either way, these are things you want to try at home, before you get out to the frigid crag.

*A crampon with straps can attach to almost any boot. A soft-soled snow boot will work for a first-timer, but it's not ideal.*

*Technical crampons can be made to fit a ski boot.*

## First-Time Ice Axes

Even though it might not seem like it, your first ice climbing trip will likely be a basic base-managed top roping outing. If that's true, ice axes will be the least important item for you to worry about. Since you can only climb one at time anyway, one pair of ice axes per pair of climber will let you take turns climbing. The arrangements that would necessitate a second pair of tools (seconding a lead climber who belays from above) would be a difficult arrangement for learning to ice climb. You can avoid that, and avoid worrying about ice tools, until you know that you want to dive into the sport.

## Kids' First Time

Equipment will be the crux of a child's first ice climbing experience, especially if the child is small. It will be nearly impossible to find a mountaineering boot to fit a small child, so ski boots might be the next best thing. Ski boots are rigid and warm, but walking to an icy crag in ski boots is a nightmare for little folks. Give a helping hand on icy and rocky approaches. Next, for certain-size feet, a crampon will not fit. The front portion of a crampon can sometimes be modified with straps and tape, but these modifications are not comfortable and they are difficult to reuse. Your preschool-aged ice climber will likely require a crafty modification of a snow boot or hiking boot, creating a stiff sole and crampon permanently attached to that sole. Last, you will have a hard time with ice axes. The weight of a full-size tool is burdensome for tiny arms, and the ax is as long as their torso. An ultra-light mountain ax hybrid, with an adjustable trigger rest, is probably the best bet.

*A child's ski boot can work with a crampon, but a light ice tool with an adjustable grip position will help the little ones make their first swings.*

I was eager to get my sons out ice climbing, but the awkward modifications needed to make the equipment work often froze their enthusiasm. I eventually realized that just playing in the snow, sliding on the icy paths, and collecting icicles was just as much fun for them as actually climbing. So, I just made ice climbing outings a time for play, and by the time their feet and arms were big enough for crampons and tools, I had conditioned some solid little ice craggers.

*A professional guide or instructor can help a first-timer access fleets of boots, crampons, and ice tools. With professional guidance and instruction, the value of a professional service adds up quickly.*
Photo courtesy of Colorado Mountain School.

If the idea of cobbling together a first-timer kit, strapping crampons over ski boots or snow boots, or borrowing random tools and crampons from a friend/mentor, all sounds too imprecise and too frugal, then hiring a certified climbing instructor or guide provides a first-timer with all the equipment needed to ice climb. It's advantageous to experience ice climbing with an ice climbing boot, to experiment with the crampons and tools one will likely purchase. A climbing school or guide service will have a fleet of boots, a fleet of ice tools and crampons, and most importantly professional instructors and guides help a first-timer learn quickly. In the end, the value proposition usually makes the cost of professional services well worth the investment, if for no other reason than access to the equipment.

# Phase 2: Assembling Your First Ice Climbing Kit

Once you've suffered the awkward learning curve of your first couple ice climbing trips, you're probably ready to make some targeted purchases that will enable you to grow and learn. Like many specialized sports, having the right equipment and apparel makes a huge difference in what an ice climbers learns (do they learn good habits or bad?) and how fast they learn (do they rapidly acquire the fitness and ability to start exploring new challenges?).

The following items will be listed in order of importance. If you are phasing in equipment purchases as time or budget allows, prioritize purchases in this order.

## Boots

Your experiment with ski boots or hiking boots should have provided some clear feedback to guide your purchasing decision. Most likely, your feet never exactly felt attached to the crampons. They were probably noisy and clanky. Your first mountaineering boot will solve most of those frustrations.

As you browse the market, the array of options is bewildering. Some boots seem to be designed specifically for ice climbing, and some boots look like modified climbing shoes with crampons permanently attached. It's confusing. Let's try to make sense of it all.

In general, for each brand, you'll see three main categories of mountaineering boots. You'll see light boots, and they look like really burly hiking boots. You'll see general mountaineering boots, designed for rock, ice, and snow climbing in most winter

*Find a model that suits your ice climbing goals and the average conditions in your area.*

conditions. Then you'll see really big boots, designed for colder climates, higher altitudes, and extreme conditions. For your first boot, that general class of mountaineering boot, that middle of the road all-rounder, is probably the best choice. Look for the signature notch in the toe and heel, and the firm shank that makes the boot stiff for steady footwork. You may find, with time and practice, that you want a lighter boot. You may find that you want a heavier boot. This middle-of-the-road boot is a good place to start.

When you purchase this boot, be sure to take some mid-weight hiking socks with you. Take advice from the sales staff, and ask lots of questions. A good sales associate will guide you to a boot that captures your heel, that doesn't restrict your circulation, that provides enough room to prevent slamming your toes into the front of the boot when you climb. If you're not confident in your choice, make sure the store has a competitive return policy. This is a purchase that you want to get right.

## Crampons

You can get away with sharing and borrowing crampons for a little while, but soon enough you will want your own. Much like boots, you'll find a wide variety of options. You will find crampons made for snow, crampons made out of lightweight materials for low-impact climbing (snow and glacier), and surgical

*A crampon with dual adjustable front points can serve you through your beginner and intermediate stages as an ice climber.*

*Crampons variety can be confusing. Select the features that align with your ice climbing goals and conditions.*

models that seem much more compact than everything else on the shelf. You'll find variable numbers of points, on the front and the bottom of the crampon. You'll find vertical front points and horizontal. It's confusing.

Much like boots, a middle-of-the-road crampon is a good place to start. Something with lots of adjustability will take you through your beginner phases and into intermediate. Something with vertical front points that can also accommodate some snow travel will be helpful. Look for a good all-rounder. There's no need to specialize just yet.

## Note on Fitting

Straight out of the box, the multiple fitting adjustments of crampons and ice axes might not be obvious. It's important to carefully read the instructions, preview online tutorials from the manufacturers, and ask questions of retail associates, professional instructors and guides, and more experienced climbers. Ill-formed modifications or adjustments can destroy expensive equipment, and that error is entirely the fault of the consumer, not the manufacturer. No matter who ends up paying for the mistake, these delays are time-consuming. It's better to put the time in on the research and homework side of things. While many nuanced adjustments and fittings will be specific to the equipment, these are the major categories of adjustment:

### Crampons

**Length of crampon.** The most obvious adjustment. The toe bail should fit snug into the groove of the boot, and the tabs on the heel of the crampon should slide right over the rugged rubber outsole.

**Type of toe bail.** Boots with a toe bail groove should take a crampon with a toe bail. If there is no groove on the toe of the boot, the toe bail can be switched out with a strap or capture that enwraps the top of the toe of the boot. For first-timers, these toe captures and straps will allow them to put a crampon on a snow boot or a hiking boot.

**Position of toe bail.** Depending on the size of the boot, the toe bail might need to be moved forward or backward. The climber will want the secondary points of the crampon aligned with the tip of the boot.

**Type of heel lever.** Similar to toe bails, the heel lever needs a grooved platform on the heel of the boot. If there is no groove, the heel lever will need to be replaced with a strap or capture to enwrap the heel of the boot. For first-timers, these heel captures and straps will allow them to put a crampon on a snow boot or a hiking boot.

**Position of heel lever.** Much like the toe bail, the heel lever can be moved forward or backward. The climber will want the rearmost portion of the heel of the boot to be directly above the rearmost points on the heel of the crampon.

**Heel leverage micro-adjustment.** Once the heel lever and toe bail are positioned, a small dial inside the heel lever adjusts the amount of applied leverage to the grooved heel platform. The leverage helps the crampons have a tight secure fit. Too much and it's difficult to put on or take off; plus you can damage the boot and/or the crampon. Too little and the crampon clanks and shifts underfoot. It can even fall off while climbing.

**Number of front points.** Many recommended crampon designs can make adjustments to the front points. An ice climber can climb with one or two front points, adding or subtracting spacers to replace a front point if it is removed.

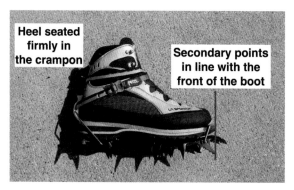

Heel seated firmly in the crampon

Secondary points in line with the front of the boot

*An appropriately fitted crampon: just the right length, front points, secondary points, leverage.*

Boot is too far forward on crampon

Heel is not seated securely in the crampon

*An ill-fitting crampon clanks and shifts. The user can bang their toes or slash their pants if the front points are too long or too short. The crampon might not even stay attached.*

**Position of front points.** Front points can be repositioned as well as added and removed. A climber can choose to wear a single front point in the middle of the front of the foot, or slightly right or left of center, under the big toe. Dual front points can be widely spaced or narrowly spaced.

**Length of front points.** Front points can also be elongated by adjusting their position forward or backward. Long front points penetrate deep, but they can pose a tripping hazard. Short front points might feel more precise, but when they are too short, the toe of the boot prevents a solid front point placement.

## Tools

**Type of pick.** Picks on ice axes can be exchanged. Some picks are easy to sharpen and slightly softer, so they work nicely on ice. Others are harder, more difficult to sharpen, and they work nicely on rock.

**Head weight.** Many tools allow the climber to add head weights allowing the tool to fall more forcefully into each placement.

**Grip size.** The size of grip can often be adjusted to accommodate larger or small hands, or bulkier and slimmer glove choices for the same-size hand.

**Hammers and adzes.** Most ice tools allow the climber to add a hammer, add a larger hammer, or add an adze. These accessories are most useful in diverse mountain travel. A hammer can be a way to add weight to the head of the tool, but sometimes a larger hammer is necessary for any actual hammering, like driving in pitons. An adze is handy for carving and sculpting snow or ice, but the pick often works just as well for small carving chores An adze can also make a

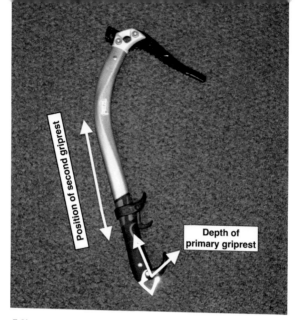

**Position of second griprest**

**Depth of primary griprest**

*Adjust the size of the grip for the hand and glove combination that will be used.*

nasty facial wound if a placement pops free of rock or ice, striking the climber in the face. Adzes are usually unnecessary for basic waterfall ice climbing.

## Ice Tools

Your first ice tools will always hold a special place in your heart. Just like boots and crampons, you'll find designs and options that bridge the gap between mountaineering, snow climbing, waterfall ice climbing, and mixed rock climbing. It's also confusing, but every manufacturer has a tool that is designed to perform adequately in waterfall ice climbing, rock, and snow. It's the middle of all the options. It's usually more affordable too, which is a bonus. Once you select

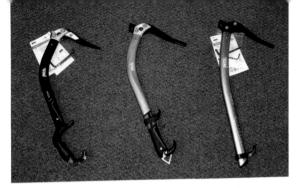

*All manufacturers produce an array of tools, from alpine ice tools to all-rounders to aggressive mixed/drytooling tools.*

the tools, you'll end up making individualized modifications that help make the tool feel like your own.

## Ice Climbing Protection

Having assembled a rock climbing rack of protection, the cost of ice screws may cause some serious sticker shock, but these are most definitely products where engineering and manufacturing excellence translates

*For a new ice climber, pick an array of ice screws that is not too cumbersome nor too advanced. Right down the middle.*

into real-world performance. One of the most conspicuous choices you'll discover when purchasing ice screws are lightweight performance ice screws versus a standard model. This theme is becoming more common among all manufacturers. One line of screws is light and more expensive, using lighter and less durable materials for the shaft of the screw and blending that with sharp steel teeth. The other line is made entirely of steel; it's heavier, but it's usually less expensive. For your first rack, the more durable, less expensive ice screws are the ones for you. Three of each size will likely get you comfortably up the kinds of ice climbs you are likely be doing in the beginning.

## Ice Climbing Accessories

**Clippers.** Ice clippers are shaped like carabiners but they are usually plastic. They look like regular carabiners, but they are only designed to carry tools and ice

*Any large non-locking carabiner can be used as makeshift ice clipper, but the harness has to fit snuggly above the climber's waist.*

*A manufactured clipper has a shelf for parking ice screws, a quick action, and secure housing on the harness so the clipper does not shift up, down, or side to side.*

screws on the side of the harness. They're inexpensive, and they're really helpful. Some ice climbers prefer to simply use a carabiner, but a well-designed ice clipper provides a place to quickly stow axes and screws.

**Repair and maintenance kit.** Once you've purchased your own equipment, the regular maintenance and repair of that equipment will be your job. You'll need some tools from a local hardware store to keep things sharp and functional. You'll need a file to sharpen tools and crampons; a big file is usually more efficient. You'll need to bring Allen keys, wrenches, and screwdrivers that accompany your tools and crampons to make adjustments. You'll need a small sewing and patch kit to repair holes torn in pants, jackets, and gloves.

Pliers and screwdrivers on a multitool

Wrenches to tighten tools and crampons

Small file for sharpening tools and crampons

A small selection of repair tools accompany climbing tools

*A few little tools will let an ice climber make impromptu repairs in the field or at home.*

# Specialized Apparel

Your snow pants and ski parkas, your winter work gloves and knit hats, that stuff got you through your first couple experiences as an ice climber, but the full retinue of pants, insulation, outerlayers, and gloves will enable you to perform athletic feats, stay warm, and bring some style and ease to your next outing.

**Pants.** You'll want to find a mid-weight soft-shell pant that stretches as you make high steps, but breaths and ventilates while you exert yourself on long climbs and approaches. Shopping for soft-shell pants is not obvious, but your rock climbing shopping will be helpful. You'll probably just want to pay attention to some critical features that differentiate an ice climbing pant from a rock climbing pant.

- Balance warmth and breathability. If the pant is too light, it'll feel great when you start to sweat, but you'll shiver once you stand still to belay. The mid-weight models will be a good place to start.

- Zippered pockets. You don't want your pockets filling with snow, ice shards, and spindrift. Look for a design where all the pockets close fully with a zipper.

- Inner calf to cuff protection. A pant that has some sturdy fabric from the inside mid-calf to the cuff will probably let you get away with a few stumbles and tears from crampons. It's a nice feature to look for.

- Internal gaiter/snow cuff. If you are in a place with deep snow, that internal snow cuff will keep snow out of your socks. These extra layers around the cuff of the pant might also decrease breathability, so make sure you need that level of protection.

**Insulation.** Just like rock climbing, those insulating layers let you pile on insulation when you're cold and strip layers off when you're too warm. A combination of non-cotton base layers and down or puffy micro-jackets usually does the trick.

*Insulation combinations can vary, but a hooded mid-weight layer and micro-puff layer are very common.*

**Jacket.** Apply the same ideas of a soft-shell pant to a soft-shell jacket. You want a layer that breaths and protects, but, when it comes to the jacket, you've got to think very carefully about how the garment fits under a harness. Some designs have a harness in mind, and they don't trap pockets where a harness will ride on the hips. Some jackets have clever cuts or features that keep the jacket from pulling up from behind the harness when the climber reaches and stretches high above their heads. Take your harness with you when you shop for a jacket.

*The right outer layer provides warmth, a full range of motion, and just the right features for an average ice climbing outing.*

*A heavy and well-insulated jacket provides a warm shelter from the weather while an ice climber is forced to stand still.*

**Belay jacket.** A large, durable puffy jacket with a hood that can extend over a helmet is a critical part of ice climbing. It's the garment you wear while belaying, setting up, or waiting to climb. A great belay jacket is your shelter from the frigid conditions of ice climbing. You hide in it when you're not climbing, and then you strip it off when it's time to hike or climb.

**Gloves.** Your glove kit is one of the most individualized. Some climber's bring as many as four or five pairs of gloves on an ice climbing outing. Most simply have two. One pair of gloves is small and more nimble. It's your climbing glove. When you are gripping your

*A two-glove system is common and advantageous for ice climbing. The lighter, more dexterous glove is used for climbing; the heavier glove is used for belaying and warmth.*

tools, moving and keeping your heart rate up, this glove is great. You sacrifice warmth for dexterity while you're climbing. But your other glove is your belay glove. It's a big, well-insulated glove that you use just like your belay jacket. You put these big, warm gloves on when your body is stationary.

**Outer layers.** Thick, waterproof pants and a waterproof shell are wise investments for an ice climber. These layers are not as breathable or

*When ice climbs are dripping with water, or when high winds batter the cliff, a set of tough waterproof outer layers save the day.*

comfortable as the soft-shell pants and jackets previously mentioned, but they are necessary when ice climbs are dripping with unfrozen water, when the wind kicks up, or when really cold conditions necessitate an unexpected outer layer. The ultralight rain gear that one might stuff into the bottom of a rock climbing kit is not the right stuff either. The more durable waterproof fabrics are thicker and more expensive.

## Ice Climbing Conversions

**Harness.** There are a variety of other miscellaneous applications that many ice climbers choose to make to their rock climbing gear. For example, if your climbing harness doesn't fit the same way when you wear extra clothes and extra layers, then consider purchasing a harness that is used entirely for ice, and sized for those layers. Consider moving from fixed leg loops to adjustable leg loops, from a one-buckle waist belt to two buckles. Whatever makes that harness fit just right with your average ice climbing layers.

**Helmet.** Many ice climbers discover that the constant icefall from above necessitates a harder more durable helmet. While their ultralight rock climbing helmet might feel like a feathered cap on warm rock climbing days, it tends to take a beating on ice climbing days. Converting to a hard-shell helmet might mean less frequent replacements.

**Soft goods.** Many ice climbers convert their rock climbing nylon into ice climbing UHMWPs, like spectra or Dyneema™. Nylon shoulder-length slings are exchanged for Dyneema™. Long nylon cordelette can be exchanged for a quadruple-length Dyneema™ sling, 240cm in length. Ultra-high-molecular-weight polymers don't absorb water like nylon, so they tend not to freeze and stiffen.

**Backpack.** Many rock climbers modify their backpacks for ice climbing outings, or they purchase a separate pack with unique ice climbing features. Importantly, ice ax loops will allow a climber to transport ice axes, cleanly strapped to the outside of the

*An ice climbing pack has a few key features that are unique: ice ax loops, a place to strap crampons outside the pack, and enough volume for extra clothing, thermos, repair kit, etc.*

pack. A length of bungee cord and closure toggle laced through the outside the pack will allow an ice climber to transport snow-covered crampons on the outside of the pack. It's a simple and inexpensive modification.

**First aid kit.** A rock climber's first aid kit can easily do double duty as an ice climbers first aid kit. However, it is often wise to augment the trauma care capacity of a first aid kit, since ice climbing can potentially involves more lacerations and trauma from icefall or impalements by tools and crampons. It's a good idea to add a little extra gauze, a SAM splint, and some butterfly closures to an ice climbing first aid kit.

## Creature Comforts

**Thermos and hot drink.** An ice climber's creature comforts are slightly different than a rock climber's. While a rock climber might be perfectly happy to drink water, an ice climber might be happier with the service of a hot drink. Sugary hot beverages like hot chocolate allow an ice climber a warm refreshment and a sugary boost to their metabolism. That means that a durable, tightly sealed, and well-insulated thermos is a vital part of the ice climbing kit.

**Food and snacks.** Food is an interesting challenge in freezing conditions. Many food items freeze, making them either inedible or unpleasant. Think carefully about that. Replace your ham and tomato sandwich with peanut butter and jelly. Avoid bars and candies that will freeze solid and be difficult to eat, or appreciate that you may have to warm those items by storing them next to your body for 5 minutes.

**Hand and foot warmers.** A few hand warmers in the pockets, or stuffed into belay gloves or footwear can mean the difference between numb, immobile digits and a pianist's dexterity.

**Handkerchief.** For many, cold days come with a steadily running nose, and a small handkerchief is the way to go for those regular wipes and sniffles. Paper products, like Kleenex or paper towels won't last very long, whereas a soft cotton handkerchief, stored close to the body, can be kept dry and unfrozen for the routine schnoz maintenance cold days require.

**Sun and wind protection.** An ice climber will also renew their appreciation of old necessities from rock climbing. The sun can be particularly harsh in snowy and icy conditions, reflecting off of those frozen surfaces and burning parts of the face that one never expected. As a result, sunscreen, sunglasses, and lip balm are staples of the ice climbing world. They're also handy accessories and forethought in windy conditions, but a face guard will likely provide more substantial protection from wind. Scarves end up being too dangly, and various neoprene face masks have an odd look to them. Instead, try using neck gaiters, more than one even, to cover the nose and face. They're remarkably versatile little garments.

## Phase 3: Ice Climbing Specialist

Once you catch the ice climbing bug fully, you can diversify and specialize your equipment into the categories that interest you most. While our recommendations for the middle of the road products are appropriate for your first ice climbing kit, specialized items are the natural progression and deviation from those generalizable products. The list could get exhaustive, but we'll list a few items that are really common.

**Aggressive/advanced ice tools.** The oddly shaped ice tools with multiple gripping pommels and triggers are designed for steep, overhanging ice, and they are particularly well suited for mixed rock and ice climbing, and drytooling. Usually, an ice climber is pretty far along before the bells and whistles of these higher-end tools come in handy. If you're finding yourself up and down hanging daggers, under and over curtains, or full on rock drytooling, you've probably at least tried a pair of these tools, borrowing them from a friend. Once you have more than one pair of ice axes, you know you've gone down the ice climbing rabbit hole, so don't purchase these tools too early, and don't purchase them unless you want to go where they will take you.

**Minimalist crampons.** An all-around crampon works in an all-around way: great on waterfall ice, great on low-angled ice, great on snow, great on rock; but on steeper and more difficult ice climbs, it becomes quickly apparent that the front and

*Adjusting to the mono-front-point is something intermediate climbers should eventually try. One front point can be advantageous on delicate ice or rock.*

secondary points do a lot of the climbing work. A handful of crampon models shave crampons down to the very minimal array of points needed to climb steep ice and rock. For most, a quick adjustment of their two-point crampons to a single front point is all the minimalism they'll ever require. For others, a trip to the shop to purchase new crampons with minimal design might be the way forward.

**Lighter or heavier boots.** Once you've spent some time in a basic mountaineering boot, you can make an informed decision about where to go from there. Maybe you've been cold, so you'll want to try a heavier boot, a boot that encloses the lacing system with a zippered outer gaiter, a boot with a snow gaiter at the cuff. Maybe you've felt clunky and you want to feel more nimble on harder climbs, so you'll want to try a slimmer boot with more of a performance profile. Much like owning multiple pairs of rock climbing shoes, owning more than one pair of ice climbing boots is a sign that you're planning to spend more time doing this sport. Make sure to make those purchases wisely.

**Lighter protection and hardware.** Having learned on standard ice screws and the array of carabiners and hardware carried over from rock climbing, a more experienced ice climber can begin systematically replacing their rock climbing gear with lighter more performance-oriented items. In rock climbing, it's a little harder to make this transition, because the rock environment brutalizes less durable equipment. By contrast, ice and snow environments can be more forgiving on lightweight carabiners. Lightweight ice screws can be babied by a practiced hand. The added costs of these items is offset by practiced usage, so they don't wear out prematurely.

# CHAPTER FOUR

# Interpreting Ice

Ice climbing movement is akin to rock climbing movement in key ways. An ice climber needs physical stamina to move continuously upwards, and most rock climbers have an advantage as they make their transition from rock to ice. Similarly, ice climbing requires a climber to intuitively transfer weight from one foot to the other, using footing and large muscle groups in the legs to drive the climber upwards. An ice climber must be acutely aware of the relationship between the upper extremities and lower extremities and how minute changes in hand or foot position can alter one's center of gravity.

All these movement principles are essential to the ice climber, and yet ice climbing movement feels alien and unnatural, mostly because it is entirely unnatural to climb ice. Unlike rock climbing, in which our climbing shoes and chalk merely amplify the essential movement instinct, ice is unclimbable without ice climbing tools. Crampons on the feet necessitate unnatural and unfamiliar locomotion. Ice tools in the hands have to be wielded with enough force to penetrate frozen-solid surfaces, and they also have to be clung to. The body must enable the legs and feet to kick, the hands and arms to swing, but it must also sustain the rebounding energy conveyed through successive impacts upon the climbing surface.

Furthermore, tools and limbs cannot simply swing and kick indiscriminately, the climber must read the flows and trickles that await, finding placements in the ice that are both strong enough to hold the climber's body weight, but also requiring the least amount of energy to penetrate.

In a typical rock climbing sequence, the climber reads the feature(s) in front, interprets the movement required based on what they see, and then executes that movement as efficiently as possible. They may have to improvise unforeseen movements, may have to change plans, but usually won't spend as much mental energy deciding which holds to use as their ice climbing counterpart. The availability of the hold is usually the main selection criteria. By contrast, ice climbing crampons and tools make almost any hold an option. The ice climber must choose the best option among many, while also interpreting the ice in order to interpret the move.

In this chapter, we'll learn to interpret waterfall ice in order derive some essential movement strategies

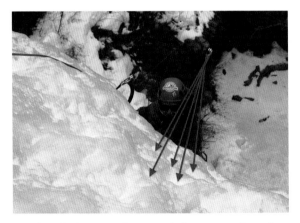

*The ice climber can place a tool almost anywhere, but some placements will require less energy, some will facilitate movement, and some will minimize icefall.*

and techniques. We'll spend a great deal of time exploring different forms of waterfall ice and how those forms are opportunities to place crampons or ice tools. We'll also anticipate the entire movement sequence as an integration of ice interpretation, reading opportunities, and weaknesses in the waterfall ice, and how the ice we see translates to the moves we do.

## Interpreting Waterfall Ice

Understanding what the ice is, whether it's wet and soft, hard and brittle, or heavily chopped and travelled by previous climbers, has value, but that value is lost if the climber does not also perceive how tools might be swung into those variations, and how crampons might stand on them.

No matter what you're doing, swinging tools or kicking crampons, an ice climber will see six distinct characteristics of waterfall ice: the plane of the ice relative to the climber's eyes, the steepness of the ice relative to the climber's feet, the brittleness of the ice, signs of previous travel, and the life cycle of the ice. Amazingly, the ability to see all these attributes quickly, to interpret them in a single glance, is what experienced ice climbers do intuitively. A climber will need to see lots of ice, on lots of different days, in lots of different conditions to hone these instincts. It's important to stay patient, curious, and attentive.

### Plane

We tend to theorize ice climbing in flat geometric planes, but nature rarely constructs anything that has any such industrial regularity. Ice undulates and bulges. It forms columns and curves, sweeping globes,

*Imagine plane as vertical and deviations of plane as angling toward and away from the climber.*

concavities and convexities. An ice climber must learn to make two simultaneous estimations. At a glance, they must blur the resolution of all these various planes of ice, and average out everything their eyes might otherwise perceive. They must say, the plane of that part of the ice, in general, is facing right, or left, or in some general direction. To read an entire flow, they'll need to imagine an average homogeneity.

*Perceiving changes in plane, especially converging planes, enables an ice climber to find stems.*

A moment later, they'll need to ignore their imagined averages. They need to refine the resolution of what they're seeing, and focus on a single dimple, or crater, or disturbance of any plane of ice. Disturbances show them both where to kick and where not to kick, opportunities for effortless swings or endless bludgeons.

The biggest reason to perceive changes in plane is because converging planes, as in an open book feature on rock, create opportunities to stem. Stemming often provides a much-needed foundation for distributing weight to one's feet. Diverging planes, as on an arête feature in rock, make the feet narrow in ice climbing.

We can heel hook as easily or compress and arête. We must pigeon-toe narrow footing, which makes it harder to distribute weight to the feet.

## *Steepness*

Much like the plane of the ice, an ice climber perceives both an average steepness and portions of an ice flow that protrude from all the surrounding planes.

**Profile Representation**

*It's easy to imagine steepness as a horizontal plane and distortions from a horizontal plane.*

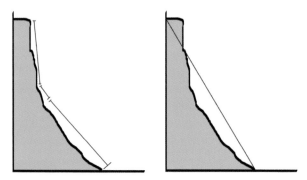

*Very few ice climbs are consistently steep. Steepness varies in a single pitch, creating rest points, challenging sections, and awkward top outs.*

On average, the steepness of an ice flow can be measured by striking a bearing from the top of a climb to its base and measuring the degrees of variation from a horizontal plane at the base of the climb. In sections, a climber might imagine that each change in steepness constituting a mini-pitch, and the same calculation from the horizontal "bottom" of this mini-pitch would convey the steepness of this section. In its own way, steepness is just another kind of plane.

## Brittleness

Brittleness is perceptible if you know what you are looking for. Ice that looks dry and smooth, especially on really cold days, will display the cracks and strain of the cold. Ice tools and crampons simply exacerbate that weakness. In brittle ice, a climber can expect to do more work for every swing, since each swing will likely displace layers of brittle and splintered ice. Similarly, crampons may need to do quite a bit excavation before landing on footing that assures the following moves. By contrast, when the ice is soft and inviting,

*A climber can tell when ice is soft. If the ice looks wet and the air temperature is near freezing, the ice is likely soft.*

it looks that way. It can be slushy soft, swallowing the entire pick or the entire front point with minimal effort. Warmer air temperatures, recently freezing water, or water that is actively in the process of freezing all looks wet. It glistens, and it's usually the opposite of brittle.

## Thickness

The thickness of the ice is perceptible. If the climber cannot see rock, only bulging mounds of deep blue and white ice, the ice is thick. If a climber can sink an ice tool all the way in to the ice, all the way to its hilt, the ice is at least 6 inches thick. By contrast, if a climber can see through the ice, see through its transparent and thin layers to the rock beneath, the ice is thin. When the ice is thin, the pick of an ice tool or front points can penetrate all the way through the thin layer and bang against the rock underneath.

## Signs of Previous Travel

Each climber will make a physical impact on the ice climbing surface. It's unavoidable. It's a much different

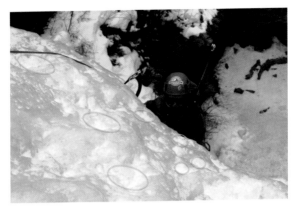

*Signs of a few previous tool placements can be subtle.*

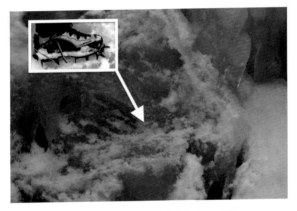

*Someone has been carving a mini-ledge with crampons here.*

experience to be the first climber on an icefall, versus the five-hundredth. Most of us will be somewhere in between when our turn to climb comes along, so the signs of other ice climbers should be there for us. The first ice ax swing that penetrates a plane of ice shears off the angle of that plane's steepness, and each

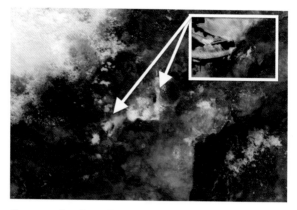

*Someone has been front pointing here.*

subsequent swing deepens that relief. After so many dozens of swings, the successive blows create a mini-ledge or bucket. These baseball-size craters can be so deep that ice tools simply hook into them. Crampons create similar impacts, but they are usually not as deep and they don't form as rapidly.

## The Life Cycle of the Ice

As ice freezes and sits through so many cycles of warm and cold, an ice climber will learn to recognize various indications of the ice's life cycle. Forming ice has the wet luster that is so distinguishable, and the sluggish waves of water are captured in this initial freeze. In time, these ripples will smooth into a single smooth plane, deep and bluish. The sun and radiant heat pocks the surface of the ice with aeriated crystals, and warmer conditions bring a melting sheen onto that surface. Columns form when drips or runnels form a stalactite from above (an icicle) and stalagmite from

*Freezing drips form icicles, and they are answered by rising cones. When they connect, they form a column.*

below (an ice cone). Once these converging features connect, the column can swell and fatten in all directions. Snow can also throw and interested life event into ice. Once it falls, it usually blows away in the wind, or it's swept away by foot traffic. Occasionally, snow will fall on a section that is still actively raining

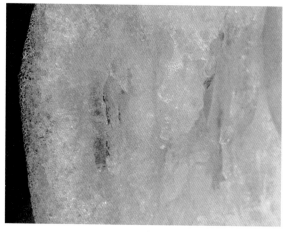

*New soft ice*

liquid water from above, and this water can form a crust on top of the snow. Beneath that crust, the white wet snow discolors all the ice that forms above, making it seem white and opaque. The snow-ice combination is often referred to as "snice."

## *Tips for Ongoing Practice*

Reading and interpreting ice does not require any exposure to risk. Ice climbers can observe and scout ice like a birdwatcher watches birds. It is pleasant and intriguing to simply go into the field and look at all the different kinds of ice, taking notes and photos, in much the same fashion as a field biologist would observe an animal species. As you do, take note of what you saw, what the conditions were when you saw it, and capture an image. Learning to ice climb is about learning ice, and you can become a student of ice without any experience, climbing partners, or climbing equipment.

| What I observed... | Time of day | Aspect of formation | Cloud cover | Air temperature | Recent weather events (high temps, low temps, snow) | Thickness or diameter |
|---|---|---|---|---|---|---|
| Wet soft ice | | | | | | |
| Dry brittle ice | | | | | | |
| Aeriated ice | | | | | | |
| Sun-baked ice | | | | | | |
| Columns | | | | | | |
| Icicles | | | | | | |
| Ice cones | | | | | | |
| Rime | | | | | | |
| Splash ice | | | | | | |
| Icefall/collapse | | | | | | |

# CHAPTER FIVE

# Footwork and Crampons

If staring and studying were all there was to ice climbing, we could end the chapter here, but a climber only reads ice so that she can climb it. Fundamental to every move is the placement of the climber's feet, and to place the feet means to learn to use a crampon with the same aplomb as a rock climber relies on her sticky rubber.

To start, flat-footed stances should be understood and practiced. When an ice climber stands flat on their feet, in a flat frozen creek let's say, ten downward teeth on each foot are pressed by their body weight into the frozen surface. If the ice is soft, they might not need much more pressure than their own body weight to sink these teeth into the ice and feel the security of flat-footed purchase, but if the ice is hard and brittle, they'll need make every step with a sharp downward stomp, biting the crampon's teeth into the surface. It is indeed embarrassing and frustrating to wear the most effective tool to prevent a slip on water ice and slip anyway, so learn to stomp with every step. Reading ice is important, even on flat-footed flat ice, because the interpretation of the ice surface tells the climber when to stomp and when to stroll.

It's equally embarrassing to trip on one's own pants and fall, so learn to strike a wide gait with every step.

*With all the downward points engaged, a flat-footed stance should feel restful and secure.*

Even as the ice steepens, like when hiking up a WI1 frozen creek, the ice climber tends to retain that flat-footed position. Flat-footed movement feels awkward at first, but it also strives to engage every point on the bottom of both crampons, deep enough to secure the climber. As the steepness increases, a climber may use a duck-walk technique or a step-through technique (French technique).

*With the ice ax in the cane position, the duck walk engages all downward points on both feet.*

*In the step-through technique, both feet are perpendicular to the plane of the ice, and the caned ax is in the uphill hand.*

*On the uphill step, the uphill foot angles slightly, pointing the toes downhill slightly, to firmly stomp the heel and downward points.*

*On the step through, the downhill foot passes the uphill foot, firmly plants, and the climber can begin the cycle anew.*

To descend this kind of ice, the same idea applies. All downward teeth of both crampons should secure the climber's footing. To achieve this, a climber squats slightly, bending at the knees prominently. This slightly seated position and the lower center of gravity allow the climber to stomp the feet flat into the low-angle surface as necessary.

As the ice steepens to WI2 ramps and slabs, it is often difficult to maintain the duck-walk and step through techniques. These steeper sections of low-angled ice require the ice climber to front point one foot while anchoring with a flat foot. The feet form an L-shape at the heels, and climbers know this position as third position.

In this position, the high foot kicks straight into the ice, engaging the forward facing fangs on the front of the crampon. The ice climber learns to kick

*Down climbing low-angled terrain is more like down stomping. The climber lowers her center of gravity and stomps each step.*

*In third position, the climber front points the uphill foot and uses a flat foot on the downhill foot.*

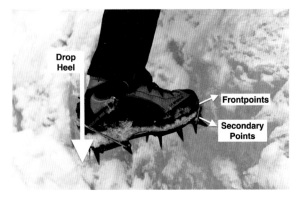

**Drop Heel**

**Frontpoints**

**Secondary Points**

*Front pointing begins with a firm kick, from the knee, stabbing the front points into the plane of the ice. A conscious drop of the heel engages the secondary points.*

the front points into the ice and then decisively drop the heel to engage the secondary points on the front of the crampon. This two-step foot motion takes repeated practice.

Many rock climbers have a difficult time learning to front point, and it's understandable. Rock climbers spend much of their timing smearing, where the forefoot maximize surface contact with the rock and the heels drop, to keep the rock climber's center of gravity poised on the smear. That's great practice for front pointing, but rock climbers also spend much of their time standing higher and higher on the tips of their toes. Trying to duplicate that motion in a crampon creates the opposite of the desired effect. The secondary points disengage, and the front points arc downwards, where they are likely to shear. If the climber is wearing a bulky boot, the toe of the boot might even make contact with the ice at this point, levering any remaining purchase of the front point right out of the ice.

*When the climber tries to stand on their toes, their secondary points disengage, and their front point is likely to shear out of the ice.*

As the ice steepens, the climber will likely need both crampons front-pointing to climb short vertical sections. It's important to experiment with wide stances, which stabilize the climber with a wide foundation, and narrow stances, which let the climber take short ascending steps with greatest economy of movement. The climber should be scanning the entire climbable surface for the most secure footing opportunities that require the least energy to achieve. Flat-footed stances are usually easier to initiate and more restful, so any ledge or horizontal relief in the climbing should be one of the first things the climber notices. Mini-ledges often have key identifiers, like accumulated snow, ice terraces, or ice debris that has landed and frozen in place.

When resorting to front pointing, it's important to look for stability in the front point placement, being careful not to kick through curtains, shatter thin ice or verglas, or snap off fragile daggers and icicles. Ideal front pointing opportunities are often revealed by solid vertical or near-vertical ice flows.

Snow, snice, and chandelier ice often present opportunities for footing, but these features/opportunities can vary in their effectiveness. Collections of soft snow can often swallow the entire foot, creating a stance that captures all the crampon points and the boot as well. Often, the security of this footing is a sought-after relief. Sometimes, the snow is so deep or so unstable that the diving foot never finds the bottom it's hoping for. Similarly, snice or thin layers of ice atop snow can either be nerve-wracking and precarious or comfortably secure. They're a gamble. Sometimes, a penetrating foot breaks right through the snice and buries into the snow beneath. Other times, the snice was the only thing holding the mini-ledge together, and the plunging boot never finds the security it was aiming for, or the ice layer is so thick the boot cannot penetrate at all, or it doesn't penetrate at first and then suddenly penetrates unexpectedly. Chandelier ice can be so brittle an ice climber can bury an entire foot into the brittle maze; the footing feels secure and sometimes it is. Other times, disappointingly, as soon as weight is transferred to this foot, the lattice all around the footing crumbles and breaks.

Occasionally, crampons can also make use of rock for footing. The downward teeth and front points cannot penetrate rock like they do ice, so an ice climber should keep an eye out for ledges, pockets, and cracks where the crampon is unlikely to shift or slide from the rock.

Lastly, it's important to understand how the crampon can be used to carve and sculpt any ice surface. WI2 slabs can be carved into flat steps. Near-vertical

*Crampon points can grab tiny rock edges or ledges for footing.*

flows can be carved into mini-ledges. It's important to remember that ice is impermanent, and it can be shaped into the footing that one desires, so long as the climber has the position and stamina to do the sculpting.

## Tips for Ongoing Practice

Most movement techniques can be practiced close to the ground and alone. Many climbers do not like to suffer their learning curve in front of other climbers. Solo ice bouldering can be the answer, but you have to know what you're looking for and you can't be tempted to venture too far from the ground. In general, ice bouldering should not explore higher than a body length above the landing zone, and the landing zone should be flat and forgiven, a nice pillow of snow would be ideal.

| Crampon techniques | Where to practice |
|---|---|
| Flat footing | Flat or nearly flat ice |
| Duck footing | Gently uphill-sloping ice up to 20 degrees |
| One flat foot, one front point | Ice slabs up to 50 degrees |
| Two front points | Vertical or nearly vertical ice 50–90 degrees |

# CHAPTER SIX

# Using Ice Tools

E very placement of a crampon is answered or preceded by some placement of an ice ax, when climbing ice. In WI1 and WI2 climbing, the ax is mostly used as a cane, like how one might use a walking stick to resist the desire to take one's weight off of one's feet, keeping the center of gravity firmly engaging the downward teeth of the crampon.

*When the ice is low angled, the climber is mostly upright, standing on both feet, so an ax is most useful in the cane position.*

By the time a climber encounters WI3 ice climbs, the tool's reverse-curve picks and the handles of the tool are used to create deep friendly jugs anywhere a climber needs one. The position where the pick is firmly planted and the handle is being pulled straight down is called the traction position.

*A traction position allows the climber to pull straight down on the tools handle.*

A well-placed tool in traction position is effectively a ladder rung. It's hard to imagine a better hold. A rock climber will be especially appreciative of a hold this good. But it comes at a price. A hold this good has to be forged with clear wits and an assertive swing. To create that swing, a climber swings the tool from the elbow using a well-timed flick of the wrist to create enough head speed to sink the pick firmly into the ice. Modulating the force of a swing so that it's just enough, never too much or too little, takes practice.

To remove a tool, the reverse curve of the ice ax pick performs its role. An outward prying motion on the handle of the tool cuts and widens the pick placement, so that it can be lifted straight up and out. Easing the difficulty in tool removal is another key reason to modulate the force of one's swing. Unnecessarily deep pick placements are harder to remove.

In the traction position, most ice tools have multiple gripping positions, so that a climber can grip up higher on the tool as necessary to keep moving up a climb.

*The climber targets where he wants the pick of the ax to land, swings from the elbow, and uses a well-timed flick of the wrist to create the desired head speed, penetrating the plane of the ice.*

When tool placements are made directly overhead, any incidental icefall can fall directly into the climber's face. It's important to learn to look down as a sort of punctuation of every overhead swing. In that case, any falling ice will land directly on the helmet, instead of lacerating the climber's face.

*As ice falls out of an overhead placement, the climber looks down, so that falling debris lands on top of the helmet.*

While the traction position is persuasively comfortable, placing the tool can be exhausting, no matter how one modulates the force of the swing. For this reason, an ice climber craves a tool placement that

*Some deep cups of ice do not even require a swing. A climber can just hook the tool into the large feature. It's important to pull straight down on a hook.*

requires very little work. The signs of previous travel usually present opportunities where the tools can be tapped into an already deep placement with little force, or the crater left by previous climbers might be

*Rock features can be hooked just like ice features. Again, be careful to pull straight down.*

so deep it requires no swing at all. In these placements, an ice climber can take full advantage of a hook placement, a placement where the pick simply hooks around an object, like one might use ice tools to climb a stepladder.

Just like with crampons on rock, ice tools can also hook rock features, when they are available and convenient.

When tools are temporarily not in use, they can be stowed on ice clippers or over one's shoulder.

## Tips for Ongoing Practice

Ice bouldering is a valuable exercise for ongoing practice with ice tools. It's equally valuable to just swing the tool repeatedly, never even climbing on it. Gain a sense for what a solid connection feels like, the resonant vibrations a solid placement makes when it finds its mark. Additionally, make placements and pull on them. Gain a sense for what placements tear and shear through brittle chandeliers of ice, how placements between columns can sometimes hold but sometimes cleave between the columns. Practice removing tools quickly and sawing forward with the reverse curve of the pick.

Lastly, consider some specific strength training if it's difficult to wield the tool with authority. Don't bother with indirect weight training or the rock gym; you'll want to imagine the way Rocky Balboa would practice. Find a sturdy railway tie, tree stump, or thick, heavy piece of wood. Purchase a hammer and several hundred ten-penny nails. Practice hammering nails into the wood, with both hands, and strive to sink the nails in fewer and fewer strokes. You might not create elegant carpentry, but you will gain invaluable strength and muscle memory from this kind of training.

| Ice tool technique | Where to practice |
|---|---|
| Strength and precision | Hammering nails |
| Cane position | Any slab of ice |
| Traction position | Any vertical or near-vertical section of ice |
| Hooks on ice | Any deep cup of ice, maybe one that you create through successive swings |
| Hooks on rock | Any in-cut rock feature |

# Fundamental Movement Sequences

Saying that crampon placement and ice axe placement combine to move the entire body is definitely a simplification of complex motor skills and body mechanics. The basic movement sequences described in this section are often diversified, hybridized, and in a jam ice climbers deploy unorthodox moves to get themselves on track, into a rest, or out of harm's way. It would be naïve to imagine that ice climbers always move robotically and mechanically, and it would be equally naïve to suggest that they should attempt it. Instead, basic movement sequences help new ice climbers understand crucial ideas like movement economy, firm foundations, and how an anchored and grounded climber can make targeted and precise placements. These are the fundamental ideas that basic movement sequences engrain.

## Fundamental Movement Sequence 1: Ascending Low-Angled Ice, WI2

On these low-angled flows, the ice is too steep for continuous flat footing, so the crampons will recycle one front point and one flat foot, the dancer's third position. The climber will mostly stand upright, so one tool will likely be used in the uphill hand in the cane position. The uphill foot moves first, as it's the climber. The climber strikes a solid point, leans on the uphill caned ice ax if necessary, and then moves the flat foot up to the position of the previous front point. This flat foot anchors the climber to begin the sequence anew,

*From a flat-footed downhill foot, establish an uphill front point.*

*Shift the downhill flat foot uphill and establish a new flat foot right behind the uphill front point. This anchored flat foot allows the uphill front point to move again.*

so multiple stomps are sometimes needed to deeply embed all the downward teeth of the crampon.

If the climber needs to change feet or direction to face away from wind or move to a lower-angled section, they simply switch hands with the uphill tool, adjust their front point into a flat-footed placement, and shift their lower flat foot into the new uphill front point.

## Fundamental Movement Sequence 2: Clearing a Bulge, WI3

When a vertical bulge emerges, an ice climber will need both tools in a traction position, and both crampons will likely be front pointed throughout the sequence. The climber steps up to the vertical section and makes an initial tool placement. That handle is used to move the feet up onto the vertical flow in a wide stance. The first tool placement is pulled close into the body, the climber's bicep pulling the upper body close to the tool and bringing the climber's center of gravity directly over their feet. Many climbers have likened this widen stance and clutched arm to the way any person might try to push a heavy object. The wide stance and poised center of gravity lets the climber push. In this case, the climber is going to swing an ice tool, not push.

The climber now swings the second ice tool directly overhead, probably clearing the vertical section of the bulge and making the second tool placement on top of the bulge. There are a couple critical decisions to be made in this moment. First, the climber should be wary of tool placements on bulges. Typically, the front side of the bulge, the rounded convexity closest to the climber's face, will fracture into

Frisbee-size plates if the pick attempts to penetrate the center of the convexity. Instead, the climber should aim just behind the convexity, right where the steepness of the bulge reclines. Second, the tool placement should be made directly overheard. The center axis of a climber's body is known as the gig line, and most tool placements will be made along this line, most of the time. Off-axis placements will likely unbalance the climber, or force her to reposition her entire body to accommodate this new center.

The new tool placement can be used to reposition the feet. They both climb up and then strike a

**When the bulge is at eye level, position both tools in the traction position, near the lip of the bulge.**

new wide stance, a new foundation for another tool placement. Once the feet are secure, the previous tool placement can be removed and now replace in close

*With tools in a traction position, the feet can be placed higher and higher.*

proximity to the other tool, right on the gig line, right behind the convexity of the bulge. It's tempting to reach too high with this tool placement, but

*The tools placed near the lip of the bulge will allow the climber to get their feet up high, pulling straight out on the tools.*

*With the feet placed high, the climber will be able to step onto the top of the bulge, transitioning the traction grip into a mantle on the shaft of the ice tool.*

bulges require an ice climber to resist that temptation. Instead, the climber will want both tools in proximity, close to the front of the bulge. Now, the climber will firmly grip both traction tools, bringing the feet up

*The temptation to get the tools too high too soon folds the climber over the bulge, where he can no longer see or place his feet.*

in incremental steps, until they can front point the top of the bulge. At this delicate moment, the climber can shift weight on the feet and move one tool at a time to stand up straight atop the bulge.

# Fundamental Movement Sequence 3: Continuous Vertical Ice, WI4 and WI5

Vertical ice flows prioritize movement economy, doing fewer moves to exert less energy in order to sustain longer sections of strenuous tool placements. It starts off just like the short vertical section that might precede a bulge. The climber steps up to the vertical section and makes an initial tool placement. That handle is used to move the feet up onto the vertical flow in a wide stance. The first tool placement is pulled close to the body, the climber's bicep pulling the upper body close to the tool and bringing the climber's center of gravity directly over their feet.

They'll want this powerful foundation to swing the second tool directly overhead, on the gig line of their body. They'll use the two tool placements to incrementally move their feet up and into another wide foundational stance. They'll use the wide stance and the higher tool to remove the lower tool, pull

*Swinging the tool happens from a firm foundation, a wide stance with as much weight distributed to the feet as possible.*

*The tool is placed overhead, on the climber's center line, the gig line.*

*The traction tool allows the climber to move the feet up into a higher wide stance, pulling the tool placement close to the body.*

their weight onto their feet, and make another overhead placement on the gig line of their body, higher than the tool they are currently holding. They'll reposition their feet using both tools, moving them

*In this position, with the tool locked off and the feet in a wide foundation, the climber can place the second tool.*

*The higher tool placement can begin the sequence anew.*

up incrementally and into another wide foundational stance. Thus the pattern of vertical movement repeats itself as efficiently as possible until the climber can get to a rest, a stem, or a stance that enables them to take some weight off of the ice tools.

# Fundamental Movement Sequence 4: Traversing on Vertical Ice

To move laterally, the climber will need to learn to re-center the gig line of their body and switch hands on their tools. It's one of the more awkward sequences to learn at first. We might imagine that the sequence

*In the direction of the traverse, the first tool placement is made, off the gig line.*

*The feet are re-centered beneath this placement, creating a new foundation.*

starts with a wide foundational stance and high tool placement in the right hand. Let's imagine the climber is moving from right to left. The climber can then take the lower tool in the left hand and make an off-axis

*The opposite tool can be collected and stowed on the shoulder.*

placement to the left of their gig line. They'll use the two wide tools to incrementally move their feet up and left, striking a wide foundational stance centered underneath their left tool placement. Now they can retrieve their right tool. They'll hang the right tool over their left shoulder, place their right hand on the tool that is currently placed, and retrieve the shouldered tool with their left hand. Now they can continue the leftward progression with another left-handed, off-axis tool placement to the left of their gig line.

*The climber switches hands.*

*The climber reclaims the stowed tool to begin the sequence anew.*

There are probably half a dozen different ways to alternate hands on a tool, and the variations all involve where the unplaced tool rests while the hand switch is made on the placed tool. It can perch in the opposite thumb, go in the climber's teeth, hook over the opposite tool, so many options. Fundamentally, the variations don't change the movement sequence that much.

This book has mentioned the need for a foundation in order to make effective tool placements, and the need to lock off one tool in order to swing the other. Two critical ideas made it possible for me to apply these ideas to my overall movement, especially on harder terrain. First, the stem, and the availability of stems, was a breakthrough idea. I remember seeing an old photo of an obscure ice climb in North Carolina, thinking at the time that the demonstrated footwork had to be contrived. In fact, the climber in the photo understood the value of a good stem, and it would take me several years to understand.

On all but the hardest WI6 climbs, stems are available, and they are lifesavers. From a stem, a leader can place a screw, shake out, collect her thoughts. On steep terrain, stems are the oasis a leader is hoping will come along.

The other breakthrough was the lockoff. I overheard a guide liken a lockoff to be the way a running back carries a football, gripping the ball fiercely and relentlessly, unwilling to part with it. Reeling that lockoff tool into my chest the way I had seen Walter Payton do so many times as a kid, I had a new conception of being anchored. The tool was my anchor. But Walter Payton never overgripped the ball either. He held it the way a parent would defend an infant, firm enough to repel all encroachment, but gentle enough to coddle a midday repose.

*This photo from Rhapsody in Blue, one of the most famous ice climbs in North Carolina, shows a climber that understood the value of stemming way before I did.*

# CHAPTER EIGHT

# Top Roping Ice

Top roping ice is the best way to learn to ice climb. It's the best way to make a transition from climbing rock to climbing ice. It's hard to be more emphatic about that. Most of the accidents involving ice climbing, and the most durable resentments against the discipline, derive from climbers who never really learned the fundamental movement skills needed to climb ice efficiently and securely. As a result, someone who leads too soon can easily be involved in an accident. Someone who never really learns the movement is easily distracted and overwhelmed by the extreme cold, and the fundamental differences between climbing rock and climbing ice.

Top roping is the antidote. Top roping lets an ice climber practice low-angled movement, vertical steps and bulges, vertical faces, daggers and overhangs, and mixed rock and ice. It lets an ice climber learn the subtle differences between wet ice that is forming, wet ice that is melting, sunbaked ice, brittle cold ice, snice, chandelier ice, etc. Top roping lets an ice climber climb popular ice that has been battered by hundreds of climbers and remote untouched ice; you can be the first or the last.

In this chapter, we'll look at a few common themes among toprope venues. Setups can vary according to those venues, but there are a few distinct patterns. We'll cover the most common setups. Then, we'll cover techniques and tactics used to get more and more mileage out of a single toprope setup. Lastly, we'll cover some unique concerns for the belayer and the climber when top roping ice.

## Top Roping Venues

Top roping ice climbing venues around the country are beautiful and varied. From the famously popular Ouray Ice Park to the familiar and prominent flows on the north side of Cathedral Ledge in New Hampshire to perennial road cut climbs in the mountains of North Carolina. In every venue, the toprope team will need to access the top of the climb, make a choice about top belaying or bottom belaying, rig the anchor, get some climbing in, deconstruct the anchor, and walk off. The major distinctions from one venue to the next happen in this sequence.

Some areas access the tops of high long flows or smears that might be so long that they are difficult to toprope with a redirected toprope and counterweight belay. Some areas have simple access and egress from the top short flows, less than half a rope length, so a toproping team can easily start the day with a setup, climb tons of variations on the climb beneath that setup, and then take down the setup or move it to another ice flow. Lastly, there are some areas where the top of the ice climb is inaccessible by foot, or the access is so arduous or dangerous that it's not quite worth it. In these venues, an aspiring ice climber will need the expertise and assistance of an experienced lead climber. Once the leader establishes the toprope, the second climber can second or follow the climb. Seconding is an enormously valuable learning opportunity to any ice climber that wishes to become a lead climber themselves.

# Topsite Flows

One of the most enjoyable ice climbing experiences is accessing a long icefall from the top, setting up an anchor, having a partner lower, and belaying repeated laps on flows that can stretch as long as the climbing rope. Since these kinds of venues will only allow one climbing team to operate on the flow at a time, it's unwise (and even impolite) to access a flow from above that other climbers are simultaneously attempting to lead from below. As a result, the top pitches of famous multipitch climbs are usually not an option. On those climbs, it's difficult to know if a party is down below, beginning a long-anticipated climb, and it's equally difficult (if not impossible) to avoid interfering with their ascent. Instead, topsite flows are best if they are remote and generally inaccessible from below. Also, since the climbing activity funnels into one climber and one belayer at a time, it's also most enjoyable to do these climbs as a small team. Two climbers can enjoyably take turns climbing and belaying, but once a third or fourth climber arrives, most of the team will spend their day waiting instead of climbing.

For these venues, one of the biggest challenges can be finding the climb. When approached from above, the climb itself is usually not a navigation landmark, so the path to the top of the climb can be unobvious and obscure. It helps to get precise directions from someone who has made the approach before, reference a GPS track on a topographic map continuously, or hire a local guide or instructor to show you the way. It's not uncommon to spend an entire day looking for a climb instead of actually climbing a climb, especially if you are the first climber of the season to make the approach. After a handful of teams have

*The anchoring, lowering, belaying, and rope management should feel familiar to any rock climber.*

made their way back to a climb, there may be telltale signs of approach: footprints, flagging or signage, trail maintenance. But be careful. Many footprints were established by someone who didn't know where they were going, or they were on their way to some other objective that might be irrelevant to ice climbing.

Once you've arrived, anchoring, rope management, and belaying will configure much like it might for any day of topsite top roping.

If you're being lowered, it's wise to take an ice screw, a couple slings, and a few pieces of rock gear. These directionals can be installed while you're lowered and removed when climbing back up to them. In this way, a single anchor can serve multiple lowers.

If you're belaying, be sure to bundle up before you settle in on the anchor. You might be out in that spot for quite a while, so it's smart to put on a warm jacket, thick gloves, and have some refreshments handy.

# Typical Base Site Top Roping Flows

Scores of ice climbs can be set up simply by walking up to the top of an ice flow, constructing a rope setup, and rappelling down from the top. Anchors on these typical climbs include all the same components as one might use to set up a toprope on any rock climb: bolts, trad gear in rock, massive boulders, and trees. However, with the climbing team intentionally establishing multiple climbs off a single anchor, by using directionals, the rigging of these anchors will need to be assembled more thoughtfully. If a climbing team is attempting to use a single anchor to climb multiple vertical fall lines, an anchor that can self-adjust to variable load directions is a wise application.

When the climbing team has selected an ice climb for top roping. It's wise to position a pack or marker that is clearly visible from above. Once the team gets above the ice flow, it's difficult to translate the relationship between the cliff top terrain and the ice to be climbed. The marker down low helps the anchor builder bulls-eye the fall line they wish to establish. Additionally, when putting the marker in place, carefully examine the top of the cliffs from the base for survey trees, boulders, and cliff features that will help the anchor builder anticipate what the anchor will look like. Before hiking to the top of the cliff, the anchor builder should have a rough outline of what she thinks the anchor will look like. That outline helps the anchor builder decide what gear to carry to the top of the crag, and what gear to leave behind.

Once the team has put a marker in place at the bottom and surveyed the top of the climb to make a rough outline of what the anchor will look like, it's time to get ready to go to the top. Make sure to get

*Top roping flows can be accessed from above, a toprope thrown down, and tons of variations can be climbed on that single setup.*

full equipped for this anchor excursion. Go ahead and put a harness and helmet on, get all the anticipated anchor-building tools assembled on the harness, on a sling, or in a small pack (carabiners, slings, cords, anchor rope), make sure to bring any items you'll need to install directionals on the climbs (quickdraws, ice screws, rock gear), put your crampons on, and grab at least one ice tool.

Anyone setting up anchors for ice climbs will quickly discover how ambiguous the "cliff's edge" is on an ice climb. Often low-angled snow and ice cover the topsite, which is forgiving on a climbing rope as opposed to sharp rock edges. But it also means that an unprotected slip or fall onto the slippery surface can result in a slide all the way to the bottom. Ice climbing anchor builders guard the cliff's edge differently than rock climbers. While a rock climber can just stay away from the edge, an ice climber often has to be more careful, more methodical, and more attentive to footing and exposure to drop-offs.

Also, streams and water flows that create ice climbs can often still be running with liquid water or mud atop an ice climb. Be especially careful to keep rope and anchors out of liquid water. Wet ropes make belaying and ropecraft more difficult; a rope can also freeze, making it very difficult to use.

## Self-Adjusting Toprope Anchors.

A toprope anchor that only protect one fall line will look very similar to any rock climbing anchor. Simple cordelette anchors and static rope anchors will suffice.

More often than not, however, a toprope anchor will be needed to protect multiple fall lines.

*There's nothing new about this rig. A simple setup for a single fall line.*

Self-adjusting anchors stand out in these circumstances. On bolts, the "Quad" configuration will come in handy. If there is no question about the integrity of the bolts, a pair of shoulder-length slings with combined "Sliding X" configurations can be quick and efficient since there are no knots to untie.

*The familiar Quad finds a logical application when anchoring for multiple fall lines.*

*Dual slings create redundancy with no need to untie any knots.*

It's often easy to pre-rig all aspect of this setup from a safe and guarded place, only stepping out to the bolts at the last step, minimizing exposure to slippery ice or drop-offs.

Rope anchors require a unique adaptation of the system to achieve self-adjustability, and it's important to note that these adaptations are not that common. Many anchor builders justifiably skip these adaptations because they correctly argue that the trees and boulders that constitute their anchor can easily accommodate an unequal or inconsistent distribution of the total load. These anchor builders are primarily relying on multiple components in the anchor for security/back-up, and they accept the trade-off. Trading self-adjusting properties for overall time and efficiency is often an acceptable proposition, but once in a while, the team might not choose to make that trade. On those occasion, the strands of a rope anchor will not culminate in a single BHK masterpoint. Instead, the rigging is altered such that each leg of the anchor

*The Quad can be connected to long extensions utilizing a static anchoring rope.*

culminates in an independent connection point. On the vast majority of rope anchors, that will create two independent connection points. A Quad or dual Sliding Xs can be applied to these independent connection points in exactly the same manner as one might apply those configurations to a pair of bolts.

## Lead-Only Flows

Many single-pitch ice climbs cannot be accessed from above. To get a toprope in place on these flows, a lead climber must lead up, establish an anchor, and either top belay a following climber or lower to the ground to belay from below. As discussed, seconding and cleaning ice screws is a great way to learn to lead, but a relationship with a lead climber also opens up more terrain. If nothing else, a relationship with a lead climber is simply a practical way to access more terrain.

On these flows, a lead climber will need to access some form of permanent anchor. Most commonly, there are bolts equipped for rappelling, some permanent slings or cords left on a tree, or perennial V-threads left in the ice. A lead climber has to have some permanent or disposable point to rappel from in order to retrieve their anchor.

On rare occasions, the necessity of creating that rappel station may exist. Rock climbers should be familiar with replacing that with their own cords and slings, making an occasional offering to the climber community.

# CHAPTER NINE

# Leading Ice

As previously mentioned, an experienced trad climber will likely have experienced run-out or dangerous terrain. They will likely have confronted sections of climbing where it is necessary to dedicate all attention, skill, and courage to executing climbing movement. Leading ice requires that same level of poise and flawless execution, but an ice climber must sustain that kind of perfection for the entire lead. Without practice, it would be an unreasonable proposition.

As a result, an ice climber should focus on movement, perfecting and refining movement, before even considering leading. For this chapter, we're going to insist on a rigorous regiment of movement practice and some self-evaluation protocols that an ice climber should complete prior to leading. Additionally, much like a rock climber inches into an actual lead with practice on toprope, we'll recommend a similar approach for ice climbing.

## A Progression Toward Lead Climbing

After top roping fifty climbs, an ice climber has probably accumulated enough total mileage to start thinking seriously about building up to lead climbing. Many climbers will proudly attest to starting their lead climbing long before such a number, but the affidavit of one or two precocious leaders doesn't seem as persuasive as plain reasoning. There should not be a rush to lead. There is no real incentive to truncate the learning curve. Plus, the most candid survivors of lead-climbing accidents all tell a similar story: They never thought they would fall until the day they did.

**Deep well-placed tool**

*Ice climbing is not rock climbing. If a climber is too pumped to climb securely, the Fifi hook technique allows him rest on a tool until he can recover.*

When I first started leading ice, I did not appreciate how falling could seriously injure me. I was so accustomed to the norms of rock climbing that I tried to transfer those same risk-management strategies. In other words, when I got pumped near the top of an ice lead, I'd gamble and go for it, attempting to get to a rest before total muscle failure. Most of the time, I made it, but a few times I fell. When I shared these stories with mentors and fellow climbers, they were often impressed and incredulous that I had fallen on ice and managed to escape injury. I'm sure they didn't think I had fallen as far as I reported. Truth be told, I did take those falls, and I was stupid enough to congratulate myself for my sturdiness and my boldness.

Then, one day I was out cragging and I watched a very skilled ice climber take a very serious unexpected fall and the injuries he sustained shocked me. They were gruesome and his road to recovery was long and painful.

As I processed the experience later, I was forced to acknowledge how much hubris I had fostered in my own approach to lead climbing ice. I was not a fraction of the climber my friend had been, and if he could fall unexpectedly, I was plain stupid for flirting with such a risk. I resolved to improve my technique in order to increase my margin of error on lead, and I also learned techniques that I could use to get myself out of a jam if I ever did become so tired that falls were likely.

I resolved to avoid falling, even if it meant that I didn't get my clean onsight.

If you toprope fifty climbs before you even consider starting a progression toward lead climbing, you will likely cycle through your initial learning curve, where you fall all the time, and you will likely arrive at a modicum of proficiency, where you're climbing most of the time without falling. Instead of leaping prematurely into lead climbing at this point, it might be wise to keep top roping until an unexpected fall happens. Better to have that experience, and garner some learning from it, on a toprope, than from ping-ponging down an icefall.

After your fiftieth toprope ice climb, a few things are likely true. You probably have a strong sense of what difficulty challenges you. You probably know what difficulty you are likely to climb comfortably, without strain or hesitation. You probably have selected an arrangement of ice climbing equipment that you are happy with and that you feel a lot of ownership of. You've probably had at least one experience where you were climbing, feeling comfortable and fluid, and you unexpectedly fell. This is a perfect opportunity for some detective self-evaluation. You need to understand that unexpected fall before you can make any serious progress as a lead climber on ice.

If you answer yes to any of the questions above, you've discovered your unique training regimen. You'll want to keep top roping until you've eliminated any doubt about your abilities. If you're easily distracted, keep top roping and scrutinize your attentiveness to movement. If you're tool placements were a culprit, focus your climbing on tool placements.

You'll want to get to a point where unexpected falls no longer happen.

| When I fell... | Yes or no | What does that mean for my lead climbing? |
|---|---|---|
| I was talking to my belayer/another climber/a friend. | Yes | The social aspects of climbing can create situations where I am easily distracted. |
| | No | I might not have been susceptible to social distractions at that moment. |
| My tool slipped, pulled, or sheared. | Yes | I might want to focus on better tool placements. |
| | No | Tool placement might not have been my problem at the moment of my fall. |
| My crampon(s) slipped, pulled, or sheared. | Yes | I might want to focus on better crampon placements. |
| | No | Crampon placement might not have been my problem at the moment of my fall. |
| I was so pumped I could barely climb. | Yes | I might want to focus on lower grades or train to increase stamina. |
| | No | Stamina might not have been my problem at the moment of my fall. |
| I have no idea why it happened. | Yes | I am not actively paying attention to myself and my movement yet. |

## Seconding

You can start seconding fairly early. Seconding might overlap with one's initial fifty toprope climbs. Seconding lets you learn to do chores while you are climbing. In this case, watching a proficient lead climber,

*Following lets a climber practice stamina and multitasking, honing both skills before attempting to lead.*

watching their precise movement, taking note of where/when/how they place ices screws, and then duplicating their stances and their stamina while you second the pitch, it's all part of learning to lead oneself.

It's possible that seconding produces unexpected falls. That's okay. That's actually good news. You want to find these unexpected falls; you want to target these learning opportunities while you still have the luxury of a toprope. Use the unexpected fall self-assessment to decide what to work on, what to train, what to ask for advice and feedback. You'll want to get to a point where you do not fall unexpectedly while seconding.

## Mock Leading

Once you've refined your movement to a level where you do not fall unexpectedly, you can focus your attention on placing ice screws, reading good ice and differentiating it from bad, placing screws on both sides of your body with either hand. Let your more

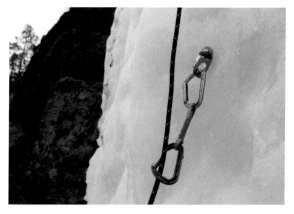

*In a vertical flow, the screw can be drilled perpendicular to the plane of the ice.*

experienced friend or instructor clean your screws, provide feedback on placement quality and ice quality, and generally summarize your performance. When your self-assessment on any skill set aligns with the feedback you are getting from your peers, mentors, or instructors, you've gotten to a place where taking the sharp end, for real, might be a reality.

*Watch out for rock underneath a slab. It can be closer than you think.*

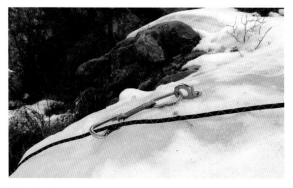

*On a bulge, avoid convexities and anchor near the back of the bulge, and don't forget to manage the rope line over bulges.*

*Large columns can be remarkably stable. Make sure they are large and well connected, in good ice. Imagine the column were a tree when evaluating size.*

# Lead Climbs You've Seconded or Mock Led

A climb that you've already seconded, with screw placements and stances that you have seen executed before, is the best place to do your first true lead. For this experience to make any sense, from a risk-management perspective, you should be climbing so well that unexpected falls no longer happen at the target difficulty. You should be placing ice screws and clipping the rope in less than one minute per protection point.

## Onsight Lead

Finally, after so much time top roping, self-evaluating, seconding an experienced leader, mock leading, and leading climbs you've already climbed, you can start to go out to places you've never seen before. Start with climbs that might seem easy or rudimentary, given the leads you have already done at this point. Selecting a slightly easier grade might be your last chance to self-evaluate. If you are hiking up those climbs, as expected, you can move on the leads that might present more of a physical challenge.

## Placing Ice Screws

Just like placing rock gear or clipping quickdraws, placing ice screws efficiently is a combination of effective climbing movement and effective technical ability. Placing ice screws is more time-consuming than most placements in rock climbing, so the stance with which an ice climber chooses to stop to place an ice screw is critical. Equally important, the ability to read the ice, to interpret dense, high-quality ice from brittle time bombs, enables an ice climber to place ice screws that might actually hold a fall.

The best stance to place an ice screw is the one that is the most restful and sustainable. On steep vertical ice, a nice wide foundation or stem, a high tool placement, and a straight-armed grip, with an available placement at waist to chest level, is usually the best a climber can manage.

On a bulge or lower-angled feature, the stance might be more variable, but in each case, at least one foot has usually found a flat or carved mini-ledge. In these stances, the climber can be so well situated on her feet that holding a tool feels unnecessary, but resist the urge to let go of both ice tools. Many climbers will attest to the occasion when crampons unexpectedly sheared free from their placements, and the only thing that arrested the climber's fall was a firmly gripped tool.

To place an ice screw, select a place where the ice looks dense, consistently solid, and connected to the larger structure of the ice flow.

*When possible, place screws in a flat-footed stance. It's more restful.*

Also, imagine how the hanger of the ice screw will need to sit flush against the ice surface. If the radius around the screw is not free from obstructions, pick a place where the ice screw can complete uninterrupted rotations. In some cases, an ice tool can be used to carve away any protrusions or convexities that might

*Strike a stance and make sure an unused tool is not in the way of the ice screw placement.*

*Get the screw started with a few twisting turns. Turn the screw in by hand at first.*

*Once the screw can stand in the ice with stability, on its own, use the spinning knob to wind the screw in as quickly as possible.*

*A quickdraw or alpine draw connects the climbing rope to the screw.*

prevent ice screw placements. But, in general, a flat plane, roughly 4 inches by 4 inches, should provide adequate seating for an ice screw.

# CHAPTER TEN

# Horizons

By the time one has moved through all the recommended progressions and learning in this book, so many new horizons open up. Ice flows of all shapes and sizes await, and a proficient single-pitch ice climber and leader will have a prime skill set to become a multipitch ice climber, even an alpinist. It's important not to rush or underestimate the risks involved in more complex objectives in winter.

In this book, we intentionally avoided hazards created by avalanche conditions and terrain. We avoided discussing big mountain objectives, whose snow, rock, glaciers, altitude, and remote exposure present innumerable challenges and obstacles. The reader should not infer that those objectives are not worthwhile, or that they are not rewarding, quite the opposite. By the time a reader finishes this book, we hope those objectives are starting to pique the reader's intrigue and curiosity.

The mountains demand great respect. Only the most deliberate and intentional progressions from one skill set to the next can give a climber any credible confidence that their endeavors are prudent, or that the outcome will be favorable. The ability to climb waterfall ice is just a building block.

# Multipitch Ice

A proficient single-pitch ice climber is definitely capable of climbing multipitch, but there are a handful of skills that will need ground schooling, team work, or professional guidance or instruction to acquire. Specifically, anchoring with ice screws, v-threading, climbing with a backpack and enough gear to survive and/ or help your partner survive an unexpected incident: These skills are not intuitive and they don't translate directly from rock climbing. So don't rush. Be patient, find good mentors and teachers, study and practice in places that don't expose the climbing team.

# Alpinism

If adventurous alpine objectives are calling, consider hiring a professional guide to go out there and provide a great technical adventure. Certainly, the adventure will be worth your time, but the true value of a professional guide is disrupting any lurking illusions about the skills responsible alpinism will require. That day with a guide will help you see all the categories of learnings that this book could not cover. You'll emerge from your adventure with a strong impression of responsible alpinism and a checklist of new study and learning.

- Take some avalanche education. Learn about group travel, decision making, planning and preparation, and emergency preparedness and response.

- Take a class on snow climbing and anchoring.

- Learn more about mountain weather, including field forecasting.

- Follow any specific recommendations from your guide.

## Mixed Climbing

If mountain and multipitch adventures don't capture your imagination, then consider exploring more mixed rock and ice climbing. Even in a single-pitch setting, mixed climbing uncovers a world of new challenges. In this book, we stipulated that minimal mixed climbing is involved in most waterfall ice climbing. While we believe that's true, once mixed climbing and drytooling are added to the mix, winter climbing has a whole new range of possibilities.

No matter what comes next, ice climbing will always be here, it will always be rewarding, and there are countless days to be had on single-pitch ice climbs around the world. Have fun and be careful.

# Sharpening Ice Tools and Crampons

When sharpening tools, try to recreate the angles and shape of the manufactured pick. It will take patience to slowly file away metal that has dulled or been bashed flat by unintended impacts with rock. If it's difficult to tuck the tool under one arm to keep it steady, consider removing the pick at home and clamping the pick into a table vise.

Front points can be very difficult to sharpen without a table vise. Consider removing the front points and using a vise to keep them steady. Otherwise, place

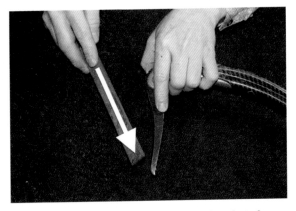

*Sharpen the pick with steady one-directional strokes, recreating the angles and planes of the original manufacture.*

the crampons on the edge of a counter (be sure to protect the counter with a study piece of wood) and sharpen the front points in the same manner as a pick, attempting to duplicate the manufactured shape, angle, and planes of the front points.

Sharpening downward points on a crampon requires especial patience. It's difficult to put an entire crampon in a table vise, so the crampon must be held or pressed against a flat surface. This instability results

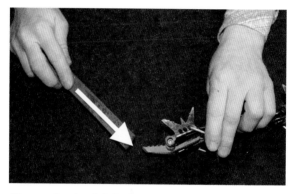

*Sharpen front points in the same manner as ice picks. A table vise helps.*

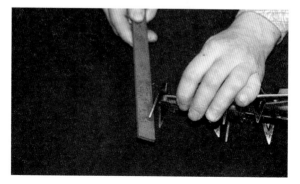

*Downward crampon points require patience.*

in more filing and requires more patience. Frustrat-ingly, these downward points are often dulled by walking on rocks or dirt, so don't feel compelled to sharpen all of these points all the time. Put in a patient sharpening every so often while binge watching a new show.

# Planning and Preparation Checklists

Taking careful forecast and route research notes allows the climbing team to bring vital information into the planning and preparation process. Cold and windy forecasts have an immediate impact on where the team goes, what they bring with them, how long they intend to be there, and what they intend to climb.

| Weather Forecast Notes | |
|---|---|
| High and low temperatures | |
| Time of day for highest temperature | |
| Time of day for lowest temperature | |
| Chance of precipitation | |
| Time(s) of day when chance of precipitation is highest | |
| Type of precipitation | |
| Time of sunrise and sunset | |
| Cloud cover | |
| Wind direction and speed | |
| Chance of thunderstorm | |

| Aspect Notes | |
|---|---|
| Aspect of approach | |
| Aspect of climb | |
| Aspect of descent | |

| Crowd Notes | |
|---|---|
| Quality rating | |
| Calendar date (weekend or holiday) | |
| Local flashpoint (events, recent national features, new publications) | |

# Hiring an Ice Climbing Guide or Instructor

There are many professional services out there eager to teach you how to ice climb. From the look of their websites, they all seem qualified and impressive. While many of them are great people and great teachers, one standard differentiates a qualified ice climbing guide or instructor above most others: American Mountain Guides Association (AMGA) training and certifications. There are many skilled ice climbing guides and instructors out there that are not AMGA trained and certified, but their skills are not validated by any third party, nationally or internationally. You have to take their word for it. AMGA-trained and -certified guides, by contrast, have been taught and tested according to historical national and international standards. Their credentials are self-explanatory because those standards precede reputation or recommendation. Reputation and recommendation are how AMGA-certified guides compete with one another, and those criteria are best deployed once you've narrowed your selection down to guides and instructors that are undoubtedly qualified to teach you.

Among AMGA-trained and -certified guides, IFMGA guides (American Mountain Guides), AMGA Alpine Guides, and AMGA Ice Instructors are the

*Any guide using this logo to advertise or indicate their credentials is well qualified to teach any kind of climbing, ice climbing included.*

*Any guide using this logo is qualified to teach anything related to alpine climbing, ice climbing included.*

*Any instructor sporting this logo passed a special ice climbing instructor exam, and they've proven themselves to be skilled ice climbing instructors.*

most qualified to teach ice climbing and guide ice climbing objectives.

Also, a climbing school or guide service that has been accredited by the AMGA provides the highest caliber of ice climbing instruction and ice guiding. Most of the guides in an accredited company are AMGA trained and certified for all disciplines that they teach, ice climbing included.

# About the Author

**Ron Funderburke** is an AMGA-certified guide. He is the AMGA SPI discipline coordinator, the education manager at the American Alpine Club, and a senior climbing specialist with the North Carolina Outward Bound School. Ron lives in Golden, Colorado, with his wife and sons.

## How to Climb Series

*Climbing: From First-Timer to Gym Climber*
*Climbing: From Gym to Rock*
*Climbing: From Toproping to Sport*
*Climbing: From Sport to Traditional Climbing*
*Climbing: From Single Pitch to Multipitch*